A 4F Goes to War

With the 100th Infantry Division

John C. Angier III

MILITARY MONOGRAPH 225
BENNINGTON, VERMONT
2013

First Edition published in 1997 by the Merriam Press

Sixth Edition (2013)

Copyright © 1997 by John C. Angier III
Book design by Ray Merriam
Additional material copyright of named contributors.

All rights reserved.
No part of this book may be used or reproduced in any manner whatsoever without written permission, except in the case of brief quotations embodied in critical articles or reviews.

WARNING
The unauthorized reproduction or distribution of this copyrighted work is illegal. Criminal copyright infringement, including infringement without monetary gain, is investigated by the FBI and is punishable by up to five years in federal prison and a fine of $250,000.

The views expressed are solely those of the author.

ISBN 978-1483901145
Merriam Press #MM225-P

This work was designed, produced, and published in
the United States of America by the

Merriam Press
133 Elm Street Suite 3R
Bennington VT 05201

E-mail: ray@merriam-press.com
Web site: merriam-press.com

The Merriam Press publishes new manuscripts on historical subjects, especially military history and with an emphasis on World War II, as well as reprinting previously published works, including reports, documents, manuals, articles and other materials on historical topics.

Contents

On the Rear Cover

DRAWING by U.S. Army war artist Sgt. Howard Brodie of an American infantryman in Europe at the end of the war.

Dedication

THIS book is dedicated to Lou, who with complete devotion, loyalty, love and concern, was my angel, companion and friend during times of severe crisis.

Also to the forgotten and unsung heroes in the front line, the infantryman, the grunt both living and those left over there. I shall never forget.

—John C. Angier III

I AM READY

The Rifleman

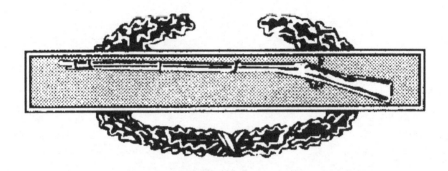

THE rifleman fights without promise of either reward or relief. Behind every river there's another hill—and behind that hill, another river.

After weeks or months in the line only a wound can offer him the comfort of safety, shelter, and a bed.

Those who are left to fight, fight on, evading death but knowing that with each day of evasion they have exhausted one more chance for survival. Sooner or later, unless victory comes this chase must end on the litter or in the grave.

—General Omar Bradley

Chapter 1

Making Men from Boys

IT wasn't until I was turned down for the Navy that I realized that I was nothing but cannon fodder for the Army. I had just left school in February 1942 to go to work at a defense job in the ship yards of the great city of Baltimore and, at the time, I didn't know whether I was coming or going. I knew that the Army would get me sooner or later, so I took an indifferent attitude toward life, trying to make the best of it until that day came.

Having left a medium-sized tobacco town in North Carolina to live and work in a metropolis such as Baltimore was something of a change and something which I was not accustomed to, I assure you. I knew a few folks there who, at the time, were very considerate. It was this small group of nice people that kept me wandering from party to party and introducing me to such fine, beautiful, entertaining young damsels, until finally I met the one. I stayed in Baltimore for about six months, maybe more, I don't remember, and by that time I had had my fill of the big city. I packed my bags, what few I had, kissed all the girls goodbye and left in a cloud of Chanel Number Five, winging my way south again.

When I returned home, naturally the first thought of an eighteen-year-old boy was to check with the Draft Board. That I did, and much to my surprise I was told that my number was coming up the following week. I don't think that this was according to Hoyle, but nevertheless I was so informed by a very dear friend of mine. I had already had my physical but had not been notified as to my classification. That didn't bother me half as much as knowing that if I were drafted I wouldn't have the same chances I would if I enlisted. Having had four years in a military prep school, I felt that my chances were better if I enlisted. That I did. Off I went to Fort Bragg with about twenty-five other men and boys, not knowing what the future had in store for me. At the time I didn't give a damn.

After wandering around the reception center, taking shots, picking up cigarettes and the like, I found myself suddenly thrown on a train, and without a word of warning, started for places unknown. There I sat with sixty other men, in a train car that was made to accommodate forty-five. Anyway, it was crowded as hell and just as hot. I heard the train whistle blow and as the train rolled along, the thump, thump, thump of the car wheels almost put me to sleep. But not quite. As I started to doze, I began wondering where I was headed and what I was going to do. Casually I thought about the type of men I would be with, what the weather would be like, and what kind of women I would meet, if any.

At ten o'clock at night two days later, we debarked from the train in a rainy, cold, desolate, muddy, God-forsaken place on top of a mountain. I spent the night on a hard, cold, cement floor of one of the new supply rooms, along with the other rats.

Early the next morning I was awakened by a loud shriek of a whistle and the unforgettable soft and sweet tone of the Sarge's voice as he calmly growled, "Get the hell off your asses and on your feet, you're paratroopers now." I sat up, shook my head, and groped for my glasses like a man trying to feel his way in the darkness, before I realized that they were going to teach me, of all people, to jump from an airplane.

It wasn't until later that day that I finally got up enough nerve to ask those muscle men from the sky what camp I was in and what town was near by. It was the most beautiful spot in

Georgia, without a doubt, Camp Toccoa; that is, if you like red mud, rain, cool, sharp air, and mountains.

Well, for three months I managed to make out with the Charles Atlas course, as I was quite a man myself. At the time I was about six feet and weighed about 205. There was no fat; all muscle and all in the right places, thanks to football and my work in the shipyards. Some of those muscle-bound babies thought they could ride me and get by with it because I had to wear glasses. I finally put a screeching halt to that one night at the PX.

I had made friends with a guy named Jack, a mountaineer from the hills of North Carolina who couldn't even write his name, but was as much of a man in size as I was. He wasn't much from the outside but brawn, although he had a heart of gold. "Jack," I said, "let's go down to the PX and have a beer and look around. Might see someone we know."

Just as I stepped up to the counter to order our beers, this bird-brain, who called himself a sergeant, came up to me with a peculiar grin on his face and a beer in his hand and said, "You are a little young for that stuff, ain't you, buddy!" I looked at Jack for a moment without saying a word. We were both thinking the same thing. Now is the time for me to take this stripe-happy guy down a few pegs.

I could tell at a glance that the beers had taken an effect on the sergeant, and thought it best that I forget it. I told him to mind his own business, and turned to drink my beer. "You want to make something of it," he said as he grabbed my shoulder and turned me around. That was enough.

In fact, it was too much for me. I told Jack to watch the beers, and proceeded to clean the floor with him. The audience was very nice, in that they moved the tables as we tussled. Jack was intently watching the other men for fear that some of them might jump me. Fortunately enough for me, they didn't; I guess they were too interested in the fight.

After a few licks here and there, I managed to maneuver him and myself into a position that finished the fight. Quick like a rabbit I lunged forward, and with my right hand under his right arm pit and my left hand between his legs, I managed to turn him and at the same time lift him above my head like a weight lifter pressing a set of barbells. I held him there a few seconds, then, with a tremendous thud, he hit the floor. Everyone was amazed, and when the sergeant came out of the fog and got his breath, he quietly went to his quarters.

About ten minutes later the MPs arrived, but it was all over, and the PX was humming as usual. Never again did I have any trouble with the good sergeant or any of his cohorts. During my three months stay at Toccoa, men wearing glasses could draw jump pay. They would merely take their glasses off before jumping, or stick them to their face with adhesive tape. Later in the month, an order came from higher up that all men wearing glasses would be shipped out to regular infantry units. Lucky for me, I was one of the first to leave under this new order. I had gotten to like the place pretty well; running up to the flag pole at the top of the hill fifty times a day, mud, more mud, working hard, good chow, but I knew it was the best thing.

Later on I was very glad I did leave. You see, I was in the 501st Parachute Battalion, and when this great outfit jumped in Africa, almost all of them were wiped out before they hit the ground. At least, that is the story that I have received from other troopers with whom I have talked from time to time.

I was sitting in the rear of a six-by-six with my duffel bag under the seat, getting ready to light a cigarette, when one of the other men asked the sergeant in charge: "Where we headed, Sarge?"

Immediately he turned to reply, and with a grin on his face and a chuckle in his voice, he replied: "You'll be going to Fort

Jackson, buddy. Seems like they are going to form another infantry division."

"Do you know what it is?" I asked, as I took a long puff on my cigarette. "The number, I mean."

"I heard the colonel down at battalion say it was the 100th, I think. You guys will be the first there except for the cadre." As he slammed the tail-gate closed, the truck moved slowly towards the train station.

On the train, most of us were pretty excited about the transfer. New faces, new places, and for me, it was nearer home. I had left my best pal, Jack, behind at Toccoa, and became a little upset about it because I had grown to know him from the ground up. He was as close to me as my own brother, but "Das ist der Krieg."

We finally reached Fort Jackson. The way the train engineer kept switching from track to track, I thought we would never get there. As I stepped off the train my first impression was a complete blank. To think that I had left all of that good rain and mud for acres and acres and acres of sand, scrub oak, and more sand! Well, I was in the Army, and what more could I expect? Anything any better than this would have surprised me so much that I would have fainted. That would have been most embarrassing, don't you think?

We managed to get off the train without getting stuck in the sand, and climbed into waiting trucks, duffel bags and all, and away we went to our new homes. We rode for about ten minutes, when suddenly the truck swerved into a street lined with tar-papered huts. The driver put on his brakes, the way all Army drivers do, and I knew this was it. Having picked myself off the floor of the truck, I heard the sergeant say, "O.K. You men wait here until we find out who's going where."

Suddenly, the truck pulled off and left us standing there covered with dust; we looked as though someone had dumped a bag of flour on our heads. Presently the sergeant returned and began calling out names. "Jackson, you go one street over, that's 'E' Company. Wait there. Anders, you stay here, this is 'F' Company, and the lieutenant in charge will be here in a minute. The rest of you guys follow me."

I took it for granted that the good sergeant was speaking to me, so I remained behind. I've been called everything from "Andrews" to "Algiers" so far in this man's Army, so I had a pretty good idea that he was speaking to me.

I waited around for a few minutes, and along came Sergeant Johnson, an old Army man who was part of the cadre from the 1st Division, then stationed at Fort Miles Standish, Massachusetts. "Is your name Angier?"

"Yes. I congratulate you, Sarge. You are the first to pronounce it correctly."

"Lieutenant Ackerhouse says to put your stuff in the hut and, as soon as you can, come up to the supply room. He wants to talk to you a minute."

I immediately did as I was told, and without unpacking a thing, I dashed to the supply room to see what the good Lieutenant wanted. As I neared the door to the supply room I slowed down to a walk, and without knocking, entered. Standing in front of me, supported by the wooden counter, was a small but handsome man about thirty-two years old.

"You wanted to see me, Sir."

"Yes," said the Lieutenant. "I understand from your records that you have had previous military experience. "Yes, sir, that is correct. I had four years at a military prep school in Virginia."

"Was that an ROTC unit?"

"Yes, sir, it was."

"Then why didn't you get a commission in the reserve?"

"Well, sir, I simply didn't go to summer camp at Fort Meade. Is that reason enough?"

"You realize that you did the wrong thing by not going to camp, don't you?"

"Yes, sir."

"We are going to need some good men around here to do a lot of instructing, teaching these new men a little about the Army, and making them the best damn soldiers in this man's Army. We're counting on you to help out a whole lot. Do you know anything about the AW's?"

"Yes, sir."

"How about your weapons? Know your close order drill, extended order and tactics?"

"Yes, sir."

Well, things went along pretty smoothly during basic training. Lieutenant Ackerhouse saw to it that I was assigned to his platoon, which I thought was very nice of him, as he was the only officer I had met. Maybe he had plans. Maybe he was going to overwork me with instruction. I didn't know what was in store, but I had made up my mind that I was going to be the best damn soldier in the whole blasted Army.

I started up the long ladder of ranks, beginning with private. A couple of weeks later, after many hours of instructing the third platoon in everything from military courtesy to field stripping a BAR (Browning Automatic Rifle), I was recommended for corporal. I gave much instruction in close order drill, PT drill, and all the rest, while the lieutenant stayed in the company area working with the Company CO. I think Lieutenant Ackerhouse had complete confidence in me, and of that one fact I was very proud.

I didn't mind the work; as a matter of fact, I loved it. I tried to be an example for my men. Everything I would ask them to do, I would also do myself. I showed them that I wasn't the type to sit back with my arms folded and tell them what to do. They liked that. Slowly but surely, I could see that group of civilians forming into an efficient fighting force, welded together in friendship, comradeship and confidence in one another. They were men learning and working together as a team to do a job that can only be done by working together. I was determined to have myself ready for combat, and as my responsibility I was going to have the third platoon ready for combat also.

During this period of adjusting myself and others to this rugged Army life, I managed to find time to ask my favorite girl in marriage. Of course, this was a very big step in my life, but I was prepared for it and thought that I could handle the responsibility without any trouble. She was a wonderful girl, full of charm and beauty, and the type of girl I thought would make a perfect mother for my children.

I sent her a wire to come to Fort Jackson as soon as possible, as I wanted to make her a Mrs. When she finally arrived, everything was all mixed up. To start the ball rolling, I couldn't get off the post to get her a room. She couldn't get one at the hotel. I was flat broke.

We were confined to the company area for nothing in particular; that's the way the Army works. I wasn't sure of getting a three-day pass, which was a very important item at this stage of the game, and because of some bird-brain idea from higher up, we all had to wear our gas masks at all times. Wasn't that something, to be married with a gas mask hanging around your neck? The Chaplain approached me, and informed me that he thought it would be all right to dispose with the mask until after the ceremony. Now, wasn't that nice? Do you suppose he actually thought that I was going to wear it? Our reception consisted of a couple of Cokes at the Service Club, while waiting for a taxi, and dancing to the music of Charlie Spivak on the juke box. The taxi finally arrived and, as things always turn out for the best, we went into a three-day seclusion at one of Columbia's more elite hotels.

A 4F GOES TO WAR

As the months passed by, the Lieutenant and myself selected our squad leaders, men who were capable of leading men, and could make decisions as situations arose. We chose the best men for our scouts, BAR teams, and assistant squad leaders, and everyone was well satisfied with all the appointments.

We kept them on the ball by giving them instruction and quizzes in military subjects that pertained to them and their squads. Our squads made very high scores on their Corps test. The third platoon made one of the highest ratings in the regiment on the platoon problem and test. We had a damned good platoon leader, so naturally we would have a good platoon. Being the platoon sergeant, I was confident that I had a good platoon. I was proud of them, and they in turn were proud, which was an excellent morale factor. Here we were, the third platoon, Company "F," 399th, which was a part of the best damned division in Uncle Sam's Army, the 100th.

Our training consisted of the usual infantry stuff like twenty-five mile hikes, RCT problems, and even guarding the Atlantic Coast Line Railroad for President Roosevelt. During these rugged months of training, I managed to become one of the first to receive the Expert Infantry Badge, selected along with Mula to attend Ranger School conducted by Rangers from Camp Forrest, Tennessee. I went to Division GAS school and became Company and Battalion GAS NCO. I became an instructor in the Nazi village, teaching men to fight in a village with live ammo.

Among all these duties, I was also selected to carry the Regimental colors for reviews and parades. This was indeed an honor, and a great big gravy train. I did manage to appear in several special events, which in turn would get me away from the everyday grind of Army training. I was selected to appear in the New York City Army Day parade, but said "to hell with that," as I had a leave coming up. I assure you that nothing was going to interfere with that.

Having been in this sand trap of South Carolina almost a year, we were sent to Tennessee for maneuvers by way of the WAC Camp at Oglethorpe, Georgia. I must say that the topographical structure of this great state was a lot different from the sand and scrub oak of South Carolina. We finally landed at a place east of Nashville called Cumberland, full of rocks and red mud. Yes, we had over 15,000 square miles of rain-soaked mud to wander in. I almost thought I was back in Toccoa, Georgia.

To me, maneuvers was the most important phase of our training. It was the phase that separated the men from the boys. I knew that the third platoon was made up of men, so I wasn't too worried as to the outcome. It was true that we were constantly wet, cold and utterly miserable. The more we suffered, the more matured mentally we became, and the more physically hardened we became, until we were hard as nails.

Day after day it rained, and the mud got sloppier and stickier. As winter set in, we were hampered with zero temperatures, hail, sleet and snow. Several days before Christmas we had just finished a problem, and were taking a well earned rest in the Cedar Forest of Lebanon. We had settled ourselves down in our wet, frozen clothes under what was supposed to be a rain-proof shelter before we got word that we could build fires. You know, you can't do things like that without orders from headquarters. We immediately began to collect all the cedar we could find for our fire and man, oh man, it not only smelt out of this world, but it was warm, something we needed badly.

After we had started several roaring fires, we proceeded to warm up, wash, shave, and clean our equipment, as good soldiers should do. Jim, our platoon guide, and I had just flopped down on our wet blankets to catch a few winks, when all of a sudden we heard several men give a loud yell. "Here's Abe with the mail." That was the last of our nap. Jim and I put on our cold wet muddy boots and slopped our way to the old man's tent.

The captain came from under his bennie long enough to grab several letters that Abe had for him. We hadn't received mail for quite some time because of the problems we were having, so I was sure that I had several letters. I only had one person who would write, my wife. She was expecting by now and I was anxious to hear some news from her. Abe reached deep down in his bag of miracles and pulled out a large box. "This is a cake for Sergeant Angier; help yourselves, men." I reached for it like a baby reaching for a toy, and told the fellows to come up to the tent for a piece.

Jim said that he would go back to the PX truck and get a case of beer. While he was wandering through the woods looking for the truck, Sol, one of the best natured boys you ever wanted to meet, came over with a package that he had just received. He had four salamis, pickles and all the rest of the stuff. When Jim returned with the beer, we had quite a party.

Neatly under the strings of my package were placed four letters of various sizes. Two were saturated with "Toujours-moi" and covered with lipstick. There was no doubt as to who they were from. One, in beautiful longhand, was from my grandmother. The last one was a long envelope with "WAR DEPT. OFFICIAL USE ONLY" in the upper left hand corner.

Having read all the news from home and knowing that I wasn't a father yet, I proceeded to ponder as to the contents of the correspondence from General Marshall's office. I was in the Army—what else do they want, blood? Slowly and cautiously I began to open the letter so as not to tear any of its contents. I read the paper carefully, then gave it to Jim to read to make sure that I was reading it correctly.

Sure enough, the Draft Board back home had finally sent me my classification and was casually informing me that I was definitely 4F, with a notation that I would never be called into the Army. At the moment, I was dumb-founded. I didn't know what to say. Here I had been in this man's Army over a year, and had done a lot more physically than was expected of the normal soldier—Ranger School, Gas School, Nazi village, Expert Infantry Badge, and numerous others. Yet I, of all people, was 4F.

"Maybe you can get out, Sarge," says Sol.

Jim says to see the captain. Brown says to go see the chaplain and get him to punch my TS card. I thought it over for a while and came up with the idea that I couldn't get out of the Army now even if I had the Lord Himself on my side. I was sure that the Captain didn't want to be bothered with trivial matters and that Brown's idea was the best. I didn't see the Chaplain, but I did get my TS card punched and left things as they were. All the guys got a big kick out of knowing that their platoon sergeant was a '4F'er, but they knew better. Suddenly my name changed to "4Fer," but I didn't mind.

Since we had walked over Hell's half-acre and part of Tennessee, I guess the big brass had decided that they, not us, had had enough. So, it was away we go in a cloud of Chanel Number Five to Fort Bragg in the land of the long leaf pine. Clean barracks, soft cots, hot showers, passes to Fayetteville, USO clubs, dances and women! Everyone was quite thrilled about the move. Who wouldn't be, after spending the winter in the open in Tennessee?

The first two or three weeks was devoted to care and cleaning of equipment and sleeping. I proceeded to get all my gear straightened out, and then went to check on the men to see that they were doing the same. We played cards, wrote letters, shot the bull and thoroughly enjoyed a well-earned rest. During off-duty hours I would find myself at the NCO club guzzling beer and eating pigs feet, the pickled kind.

After our rest period was over, we immediately went into an intense physical training program. Lord knows why, because we were all hard as nails. If the big brass wanted it that way, who were we to stop them? There was a war going on. While at Fort Bragg, we somehow got the reputation as being a spit and polish outfit, and those reputations can become an awful pain in the rump, if you know what I mean.

From time to time it seemed that the Army was using the 100th as a sort of repple-depple or something. During our stay at Fort Bragg it was said that twenty-five percent of our outfit had been used as replacements overseas to the 3rd, 36th, and the 45th Divisions, which someday the 100th would be fighting with. We only lost a few from the third platoon, and they were soon replaced with men from the Air Corps, MPs, AAA's, and the brain trust from the Army ASTP program which was folding fast from the lack of men in the fighting units. But "c'est la guerre," so the French say, and we started out training all over again, in the event we were needed across the pond.

By late September 1944, we were in Camp Kilmer POE [Point of Embarkation], keeping ourselves busy with latrine rumors as to which way we were going. First it was Alaska, then the Pacific, then England, and between the rumors, shots, inspections, wills, we had a gay time.

The only thing I could remember about the POE was that the night we had readied ourselves for the boat, it was rainy and the night was full of chill. Never have I been so outdone. Imagine men trying to maneuver around with a full field pack, overcoat, gas mask, rifle, steel helmet and half the company property on your shoulders! But that's the Army. We boarded a train and in a few minutes were unloading on the Jersey side of the Hudson for a ferry ride to the boat.

As we crossed the river, we could see the bright, flickering lights of the world's most famous city. The city was quiet, and the tall buildings looked as though they were reaching up to the heavens. As the lights in the elevators of the buildings climbed skyward, they looked as though they were lightning bugs crawling up the side of a house. In the distance we could hear the sound of boat whistles and horns, as the river was full of traffic that night.

Slowly we nestled near the dock on the New York side, and as I looked up, I could see nothing but a great mass of gray steel, a part of the USAT *George Washington*, which was to take us safely, we hoped, to faraway places. That night was our first aboard ship, and we didn't move until morning. We were packed in the ship in typical Army fashion, like sardines, with no place to sit, much less sleep.

Later that night there came a blare on the ship's intercom: "Now hear this. Now hear this. All personnel go to your compartments. All portholes and doors will be closed and remain closed until further notice." Right away, I knew that I wouldn't get a last look at the Ole Gal, so I got a good book and read until I fell asleep.

Early on the morning of 6 October, the USAT *George Washington* slid through the narrows of New York for places unknown to me, but to the skipper, he was sure of the Azores, the Big Rock, the Mediterranean, and into the ship-guttered harbor of Marseilles, in southern France.

Chapter 2

Trip Across

HOW are you making out, Sol?" I asked, as I gave him a friendly tap on the shoulder. As he tried to move his head slowly to the leeward side, I could see that this was one soldier in Uncle Sam's Army that had felt better. I tried to pep him up a little by telling him that I didn't feel so hot either.

"I feel like hell," he said, with a sickening look. "Can't seem to stop it. It comes up without a word of warni—uummpp [upchuck]. You see what I mean. This is one helluva way to fight a war. I'd rather be dead than go through this again."

"Don't worry, Sol, it won't last long. Maybe you'll feel better when the sea calms down a bit."

I wandered back to my favorite spot, between two life rafts, where I had a commanding view of the sea, to read a book and think of the days past. It was wonderful sitting there. The clean salt air blowing into my face and the continual rolling of the ship and the waves slapping the bow as we churned through the water gave a perfect atmosphere for reminiscing.

Most of my thoughts were of home, but they were broken from time to time by the sleek, gray, camouflaged destroyers zigzagging in and out between the evenly spaced transports and Victory ships. As they passed, there was an exchange of hand-waving and shouts, which were slightly heard, but there was a thought of confidence that everything was O.K. as long as they were there. It was a mighty good feeling to see that small hunk of steel and firepower cut through the convoy, keeping a watchful eye over us to make sure that we reached our destination safe-ly.

Overhead, one could hear the continual hum and drone of the motors of the Navy's great watchdogs, the blimps and PBYs. As they flew from side to side, it brought back memories of the many times I had seen this same scene in the newsreels at the Army theater at Fort Bragg. Now I was a part of it, and there was a wonderful feeling inside me as I watched the operation day after day.

Having chow on board ship is an experience I shall never for-get. There were so many men on board ship that there was only time for two meals, and one wasn't sure when those meals would be, as they changed the time every day. When chow was served, we would form a line around the ship's deck, that is, those who were able, and with mess kits in one hand and meal ticket in the other we followed the line as it descended an almost vertical ladder to the galley, as it is called in the Navy. Of course, we had to wear our Mae West life jackets at all times, and the galley was definitely not the place for such apparel.

As we slowly passed through the line, our mess kits were filled with what was supposed to be the best food in the armed services. Frankly, I don't go along with that statement, along with ten thousand other GIs. It was crowded enough with those life jackets on, much less to stand up at those small Navy tables with hundreds of other guys. One didn't know whether he would reach the table with a full mess kit or not, what with crowded conditions and the ever rolling of the ship. It didn't take long for these groundhogs of the infantry to master the situ-ation, and in a couple of days we were eating, walking and stand-ing like old salts of the sea.

Our days were spent leisurely, unless one was sick. Find a nice comfortable spot topside and write letters, play cards, or just read a good book. From time to time we were entertained by some of the ham actors, boxing matches, and most pleasing of all, good swing music from the regimental band. They were really good. Of course, gambling was out of the question. Ha; did it ever occur to you what a wonderful medium of exchange cigarettes and matches will make? I don't think much money was won or lost, but it broke the monotony and helped pass the time away. We had movies, but most everyone had seen them as the attendance was poor. King Neptune might have had something to do with it.

We all looked forward to the *Daily News*, a mimeographed sheet made by the ship's personnel. It contained the up-to-the-minute news of latest war developments and local announcements aboard ship.

My platoon was in good shape, and all were good sailors as well as good soldiers. The trip so far had been pretty good, but the worst was yet to come. On or about the seventh day out, we hit an awful storm. As a matter of fact, it was a hurricane that was reputed to be the worst in twenty years. I have never seen a ship toss as ole George did, and I must admit that I was a little afraid that we wouldn't make it. After forty-eight hours of being tossed around like a cake of soap in a bathtub, the seas calmed down enough for us to come topside for some much needed fresh air.

After it was all over, we were told of the near accident we almost had during the past storm. The ship in the convoy directly behind us had rolled and tossed within five degrees of capsizing, and it came within inches of ramming the *George Washington* right in the stern. It scares me to think of what might have happened if we were hit. There would have been one helluva mess in the middle of the ocean and a good meal for a hungry school of sharks that followed us most of the way.

Several days later, as we were sunning ourselves on deck, we noticed a terrific cloud of black smoke off our starboard side. We spent most of the day trying to guess what had happened. The story came out that night on the ship's speaker that an oil tanker had been hit by a torpedo. Then the thought struck me that we were really in the war. It was the nearest thing to actual combat that we had witnessed, and there was an air of calmness over the ship as everyone had the same thought in mind. This was it. Nearing the combat zone, submarine wolf-packs, bombers, fighters, and mines were things everyone was thinking about, wondering if we were next on the list.

On about the twelfth day we forgot all about the war, for right before our eyes, rising out of the sea like the Empire State building in Manhattan, were the shores of Africa. Nothing like we had seen in the Frank Buck pictures, but beautiful cliffs that seemed to have been painted by the Lord Himself. They were to be admired and enjoyed by everyone who looked at them. The convoy began to close up, and the Navy began to close in to signal orders as we passed the city of Tangier and entered the Straits of Gibraltar.

Silently we cruised on, sticking pretty close to the African coast, past a place called Ceuta. It looked mighty good at night. Again, just a little bit of civilization. I could see the lights blinking in the distance and wondered why they weren't blacked out. Must be a crazy world. You hear all the talk about dim-outs in the States, and you get into a combat zone and find all the cities lit up like Christmas trees.

We passed Algiers that night before turning north through the blue Mediterranean for Marseilles. We were told that we would reach Marseilles sometime the next day, if nothing happened. There were lots of things that could have happened, but they didn't.

As we neared our destination, we passed a hospital ship. A beautiful sight it was. Its whiteness stood out like an angel and its slowness showed suffering. Its bow pointed westward for home with a cargo of wounded, dead and mangled bodies; heroic men who had done their best and we were proud of them, that's for sure. That ship must have been full of interesting stories and heroic deeds which will probably never be told. The ship passing at such a time gave us the feeling and thought of: "Wonder if I'll go back home that way."

We reached the ship-guttered harbor of Marseilles, thanking the good Lord for a safe trip. We were ordered to debark in LCIs and it wasn't until late that night that my platoon started down the rope net on the side of the ship. Suddenly sirens started wailing, a smoke screen was laid over the harbor, and every light in the port was out before you could say "skin-the-cat."

I caught my breath and looked skyward as I heard the drone of airplane motors. Was this a real raid, I asked myself. Having been introduced to the ETO by none other than her Highness "Axis Sally" the night before, I was sure that it was the real thing. It turned out that it was only a German recon plane that did nothing but take a few pictures and scare the hell out of the 100th Division.

We were finally loaded into LCIs and started for shore zigzagging in and out between half-submerged ships and debris. As we reached shore, the front of the small craft was lowered and we waded on to the so-called "Shores of Southern France." Evidently the fifteen-day boat ride wasn't enough, for as soon as we hit the terra firma we had to walk a good ten miles to the assembly area outside Marseilles. In the process of unloading, we managed to get ourselves soaking wet from head to toe, and we still had ten miles ahead of us.

Although it was later than midnight, it was easy to see that there was no lipstick shortage in France, and that the dress styles were still above the knee. As we continued to grope our way in the darkness to the outskirts of the city, we could hear in the distance the rumble and roar of heavy artillery firing round after round into the southern sector along the Mediterranean coast. Little did we know that the fighting was that close. Marseilles had just been liberated in the invasion of Southern France and the Germans hadn't backed up too far.

In the pitch-black darkness, tired and wet, we reached the assembly area, not giving a damn for anything but sleep. Having settled ourselves down in an open field, covered by the sound of guns and the sight of muzzle blast, we tried to sleep.

"Hey, Jim, did you trench the tent good?"

"Yes, why?"

"It's beginning to rain. Isn't that just too too divine?"

"What a wonderful welcome these Frogs can give. First it's wading ashore, then a ten mile hike, and now rain.

"Jim, button up your end and I'll get the front. Dammit, it's coming down the middle now."

That was the beginning of our first night in France. We were located in this assembly area for about seven days, most of the time being taken up with care and cleaning of equipment and talking over last minute details of tactics and maneuvers. On the third day we had our chance to see a little of Marseilles. Passes were issued to a portion of the men, and off we went to get a first hand taste of the world-renowned wine and French gaiety that you hear so much about.

Al Mann, Finch and I took off for Marseilles for a good time. At first I was a little surprised at the city itself, as it wasn't all it was cracked up to be. The wine and liquor at the sidewalk cafes is all and more than it's cracked up to be, I can assure you.

"Hey, Al, look at those gams. And get a load of those swinging hips."

"Don't be a dope, pal; you can get better than that in sixty seconds on Third Avenue. I know."

"We going to have something to eat, or are we going to drink our supper?" I said as we sat down to a table at one of the more elite sidewalk cafes. The others didn't pay too much attention, as they were too interested in the legs passing by on a bicycle. Those French gals are something on a bicycle. They let their dresses fly up to their hips for more pedaling comfort. Mind you, I'm not complaining; in fact, I think there should be more women riding bicycles than there are.

"Don't bother us about food. It'd take all the gold in Fort Knox to buy a decent meal. Let's stick to the drinking, it tastes better."

"Tinker" and Joe had just ditched a potential shack-mate, saw us sitting at the table, and came over for a chat. They gave us a play-by-play description of what they had done so far that afternoon. We still had the night to look forward to, so we proceeded to get loaded.

"Hey, Sarge, where's the latrine?"

"I don't know, but come on we'll find it."

As we made our way through the half-vacant restaurant, I chanced to eye one of the garcons. As I engaged him in conversation with my best French and hand expressions, he finally realized that we had to go, but quick. The directions were plain as mud, coming from one who spoke no English, but as we neared the rear of the restaurant we both spotted a large sign reading "Abort Pour Hommes." This was it, we hoped. In we went and immediately, out we came.

"Hey, 'Tinker,' I think we took the wrong turn somewhere. That's for the ladies." The waiter who had given us the directions had been keeping a watchful eye on us, and came over to insure us that we had the correct door. This was where the men go, so in we went. The inside was something to behold. Before us was nothing but a hole in the floor. Nothing like the bathrooms we have at home. We began to get amused and started to laugh.

As Tinker started preparing himself, I excused myself to give him a little privacy, and stepped just outside the door. A few moments later there was a loud knock on the door and Tinker yelled: "How many francs do you have?"

"Not many, why?"

"There is no paper in here."

"What's that got to do with it?" As I handed him a fist full of francs, I heard him say: "This is all they are good for anyway." I thought the joke was pretty good and proceeded to the table to tell the rest of the fellows, forgetting the purpose of my visit to the Abort.

As the evening passed on, we did the town up right, and I mean right. Late that night the five of us started back to the open field and those comfortable wet blankets. Little did I, Al, or anybody else know that the next day was the day. Did I know that I was going to be on a truck the next day, heading for the front? No, sir, I was planning another trip to Marseilles. It seems that I was sadly mistaken.

Today was 31 October and the Eagle dropped his load in great quantities, that is, except for me. I accepted $10.00 worth of francs, and the rest went to the sweetest gal in the world back home. I knew that I wouldn't need it, so why draw it. Anything I needed I could barter for with cigarettes and chocolate. Then too, actually I didn't see anything I wanted to buy.

We got our money and at the same time were told to turn in our duffel bags and all excess junk. We proceeded to turn in all valuables that we didn't want to carry with us, and mailed them home. Most of us kept nothing but a watch and pictures of our loved ones. I sent my school class ring home and kept pictures of my wife and little daughter. This was it, and what could we do. Nothing.

As the minutes ticked away the tension grew greater and greater. The men were getting jittery and began to gather in small groups to talk in whispers and sometimes pray. Some of the more religious men were huddled in prayer, while "Rover" was telling Ballo about some gal he laid in New York before we left the States. Shortly, the prayer meeting broke up, and the men returned to cleaning their rifles.

"Jim, let's get all the squad leaders here and have a little pow-wow. The lieutenant is nowhere around, and I think that we should get together."

"O.K. Where do you want them?"

"Tell them to come to Brown's tent, that's out of the way of everything."

Later, in they came. One by one. After all had arrived I began to talk. "What's wrong with you guys? I'm ashamed of the whole damned bunch of you. You act like a bunch of recruits. Let's get right before it's too late. We have been like brothers for the past two years. We are like a team and I have the greatest confidence in all of you. I know you are afraid, but don't kid yourself, I'm afraid too. You have got to forget it 'cause we have a job to do. Who isn't afraid? Anyone who says that he isn't afraid is a damn liar. Let's not show it outwardly, but in our hearts we may act as we so desire. I know some of you are wondering about that ninety-day wonder we got back in the States. Respect him, but you know who to take your orders from. I don't know how he will turn out; we'll just have to wait and see."

I had never been in combat before, nor had the lieutenant, but the men knew me, believed me, trusted me as I did them, and they weren't too sure of him. We ate together, slept together, trained together, drank together; we became one. The third platoon, Company F, 399th Infantry.

"Are there any questions or anything anybody wants to get off his chest; if so speak up. Remember that the lives of the men in this platoon depend on how you conduct yourself in combat;

let's not screw up the works. Protect one another and fight to-gether. O.K. that's all. Get your rifles cleaned up and be ready to move out on a minute's notice."

I knew what the men were thinking and what they were afraid of, and then I realized what a problem and responsibility I had. I thought and thought and finally realized that the best thing to do was to do my dead-level best and things would be all right.

Later, when Jim and I were getting things ready, Brown, Conn, and Kamel came wandering over for a bull session. We began to talk about what it was going to be like, who would be the logical ones to screw up, and who we would have to watch. We talked about tactics and went over our own private platoon signals. The thing that put my mind at ease as to how I was going to make out, was when Conn spoke up: "We are behind you one hundred percent, Sarge, and you're boss." That made me feel mighty good and I knew then that everything was going to be O.K.

"If anything happens to me, Jim will take over. After that, Conn, then Brown, then Kamel."

"O.K."

"Luke, is that 536 working?"

"Yeah, for the time being. I don't like the damn thing, and if it's O.K. with you, Sarge, I'm going to pick up a couple of sound-powered phones and some wire. I don't think this thing is going to work worth a fiddler's fart, and I don't want my life depending on it."

The orders finally came to load up the trucks, and before I knew it we were on our way to the front. About five hundred miles later, I found the third platoon and portions of the 399th in the northwest corner of France, at the foothills of the Vosges Mountains. Fremifontaine was the name of the village, with its green rolling pastures, and thick, black pine forest. The forest was covered with vacated German foxholes; a body here and there, helmets, spent rounds and potato-mashers cluttered the ground, together with debris from old German rations, toilet paper, an old letter, and cast off medical bandages used by the wounded. There were many craters, which testified to a fierce artillery duel.

Chapter 3

Hit the Line

HAVING dismounted from the trucks, we started moving out in the old reliable way of the infantry, a column of twos on each side of the road, toward the front. We knew that we were getting closer and closer, as we passed dug-in artillery pieces and busy aid stations. On past the coughing of the big artillery guns, we began witnessing the horror of war. We passed many dead American and German soldiers. Some were still wounded and waiting to be taken to the rear. Pieces of arms and legs here and there surrounded shell holes made by the death-dealing 88's. Helmets, first aid bandages, rifles, and pack equipment cluttered the road, which told us clearly that the boys had one helluva barrage not too long ago.

We moved on, and as it was beginning to get dark we passed the emplacements of the ever coughing heavy mortars, throwing a bit of protection for the boys sweating it out up there. In the distance, we could hear the wild chatter of the machine guns, spacing their bursts to let Jerry know that they were still there and their guns were in firing order. Occasionally, the crack of a couple of M1s answered by a burst from a well-hidden burp gun, could tell one immediately that the GIs and Krauts weren't having a tea party.

We finally reached our objective for the night. This was the famous Bill Mauldin's outfit, and we were to relieve them in alphabetical order beginning that night. Surrounded by vets of Anzio and Salerno, we started the never-ending job of digging our holes for the night. No sooner had we started digging when the Krauts opened up with their 88's. Brother, that was it. Everyone jumped for their holes and prayed that they wouldn't be joined later by an 88. The Germans were noted for their accuracy with those damn things, and could put them anywhere they wanted to, even in your hip pocket, if you wanted it there. To tell you the truth, all you had to do was thumb your nose at the Krauts and turn the cheek of your rump so they could see it, and they would put it right there.

They must have known that we had arrived in that sector that night, because they really poured it on. After the first barrage we had become somewhat seasoned to the Jerry artillery, but we had yet to fight them face-to-face. That was coming later and we all knew it. Fortunately, no one was hit, and with pencil in shaky hand, most of us settled down to write what we thought was our last letter home. I had finished writing to my wife and was putting the finishing touches on our home for the night, when "Do you know how to play cribbage, Sarge?" came from the nervous lieutenant on the other side of the hole.

"No, sir, I have never learned to play the game."

"How about you, Jim?"

"Yeah, I've played a little."

"C'mon, I've got a board and a deck of cards in my bag; I'll teach you. Now the object of the game is to peg around the board."

As he proceeded to explain the game, Jim and I sensed an atmosphere of nervousness and tension in his voice, and his lips began to quiver a bit.

"What's the matter, lieutenant?"

"Nothing; I guess that barrage got the best of me."

"Now sir, you'll have to get over that sorta stuff or get out. Sure, we got a little scared too, since it was our first experience, but it's gone now. You won't last long this way. Snap out of it, you have a platoon to lead."

With that in mind, Jim and I left the good lieutenant to think it over in peace. The 399th was sandwiched between the 45th and 3rd divisions, and little did we know that the rest of the 100th was still several hundred miles behind us when we fired our first shots at the Krauts. The 3rd and 45th were badly in need of replacements and a rest, and as we had stopped to organize for the Vosges Mountains we gave them that much-needed rest.

The Vosges Mountains were the great barrier in the advance to the Rhine. The Krauts had picked an excellent place for their defensive positions, because the winter was beginning to set in and it was going to be awfully hard to knock the Jerries out of the mountains, especially with all the snow and ice.

As the 399th entered combat, the 3rd platoon, Co. "F," was already in combat. My platoon had been ordered up to secure and protect the flanks of the elements being relieved, while the rest of the 2nd Bn. was in reserve. The reserve battalion was finding that the Kraut mortars burst without warning, until they learned to hear them clear their throats with a silent but distinct cough.

As we moved up in pitch-black darkness, it started to rain, and it was getting colder every day. You could not see your hand before your face, but somehow or other I managed to get the platoon spread out and digging in for the night. Every time your shovel would hit the dirt, those damned Krauts would lob in a few mortar shells to let you know that they were still up and awake. It was miserable, wet, muddy, and cold, trying to dig a hole to protect yourself. Hell, you couldn't see a thing, much less dig a hole.

I got knee-high with my hole before it filled up with water, so, like most men in a losing battle, I gave up in disgust. I sat down in the water, threw my raincoat over my head, and proceeded to light up one cigarette after another. That is, those I could find that were dry enough to smoke. I sat there chain-smoking to keep awake, and as dawn was breaking I could see that the platoon was dispersed, much to my amazement, correctly. For our first night in combat and in total darkness I thought that it was pretty good.

As the mist of dawn rose upward, I could see a large black cliff to my front. What a hell of a place to be! All the Jerries have to do is stand up there and drop them down your throat. And that is exactly what they did, all day long. The Krauts were there all right, and according to rumor, we were to scale the cliff and take off for a town named LaSalle, which was about three miles down a German-infested road. We weren't looking for a fight. No one was—all we wanted was a little time to gather ourselves together and adjust our bodies and minds to the reality of front line fighting.

LaSalle and Remy were taken as more "firsts" were scored up for the 399th. We should have had our canoes and life jackets, as the rains began to fall again unceasingly for weeks and then turned into snow. Fighting had been pretty serious up to now, and the men welcomed a good lull, for the cold rain and snow continued to soak the ground, adding to the misery and total discomfort of every man in his hole.

Today is Saturday, November 11th, Armistice Day, a day to end all wars, so they said. Ha! What a joke! Here I sit in this wet, cold, muddy foxhole somewhere in Alsace listening to the roaring big guns back behind thundering a welcome to the twenty-sixth birthday of peace for the world. Sounds silly, doesn't it? And it was.

Sitting in our makeshift homes, everyone knew that things were a little too quiet, and that something must have been brewing, and it was. Attack! Might have known that this would happen on Sunday. It always does. Guess maybe they (the high brass) think that if they attack on Sunday and you (the cannon fodder) get hit in the process, maybe you will have a better chance of saving your soul, or something.

It snowed during the night and the ground had a beautiful blanket of the cold stuff, which made it rather hard for outpost patrols to push ahead. The 100th Division, along with the 3rd, 36th, 45th, 79th and the whole French First Army were ready to jump off. Ahead of us were the cold winter, Vosges Mountains, German 16th Inf. Div., 21st Armd. (Panzer) Div., 361st Inf. Div., and the 708th Volksgrenadier ("People's Infantry") Division.

Having celebrated peace, the Seventh Army went into action again at 0900 on the 12th, as was expected, with the grand and glorious Century Division in the lead. After awakening the Krauts with a very quiet barrage of artillery fire, a few spurts of 50's, and a couple of chatters of 30's, the First and Second Battalions led the attack to drive the bastards from their winter line in the Vosges Mountains.

We were to attack and seize the high ground north and east of Baccarat, the famous glass manufacturing center. As we proceeded along, Fox Company slugged it out and managed to overrun the German MLR, which was prepared for us to the utmost. They had zeroed in with everything they had, and their cleared avenues of fire were more than effective, for their machine guns were cleverly placed behind their log bunkers. Having accomplished our mission for the time being, we were ordered to take the high ground southwest of Neufmaisons.

The Second Battalion, with "F" Company in the lead, with the fighting Third in front, had hardly gotten out of our wet muddy holes when we were met by a hail of '88' and machine gun fire which was so intense that it took us over four hours to get our duds together and get the hell out. As we moved forward we overran the German foxholes and bunkers, which were filled with not only equipment, dead and wounded Supermen, but with a few who knew how to raise their hands and yell "Kamerad." The sons of bitches! They knew that they would get out of all this mess and be cared for, yet we were here to stay.

The snow continued to fall and it turned colder. This campaign in the Vosges was one of misery, rain, snow, and frozen fingers that couldn't button pockets or wipe themselves with a 1,000 franc note much less fire a rifle. There was a dismal, cold, mucky fog that would work its way out of the forest, changing day into a dark twilight and the nights into pitch-black darkness. All the hills were "4" something or "5" something. There isn't a dogface living today who doesn't remember at least one hill.

As we approached the outskirts of Neufmaisons, the tall steeple of the church could be seen through the snow-covered pines. We were at the edge of the woods, with a cold snow-covered field between us and the steeple. Everyone had a feeling that the Krautheads had an OP up there, and between you and me, they had some of the best damn shots in the German Army on those 88's.

It was getting late in the afternoon now, and the dull gray coldness of twilight was rapidly descending upon us. No sooner had we dug our homes for the night, when the Jerries let go with the damnedest barrage of 88's and mortars I had witnessed so far. For a solid hour and a half they came in, one at a time, two at a time and three at a time—one right after another, without letting up for one second.

I can say one thing for the Heinies, at least they gave us a little time to get ready for it. I don't believe that I had ever prayed so hard in all my life. I never knew when the next one was coming in the hole with me to shake my hand. It's an awful feeling to be sitting there helpless in a hole, hear that familiar sharp whistle, and then have the ground shake around you from the impact of those death-dealing shells. You never knew which one had your name on it. Yet you were always sure that it would be the next one. During that horrible hour and a half, I chanced to peek over the side of my hole, high enough and long enough to see ole Luke lying not three feet from me.

"Hey, ole man, you hit?"

"Hell no, I'm just restin'."

"Come on and crawl in," I yelled. At the time, I had a good foot and a half of water in the bottom of the hole, but there was always room for one more.

"Hell, Sarge, it's as safe out here as it is in a hole. Those bastards are so damn good with those fugging things that they can put them in your hip pocket in a hole as good as they can out here. I think I'll take my chances out here." With that he snuggled up closer to the base of the big pine tree, and began to light up a wet smoke he took from his cartridge belt.

At the same time, the Krautheads had a different idea. They let go with about six or eight fast ones that hit their mark around ole Luke and me. To my amazement, the lieutenant, who had crawled slowly from his hole during the shelling, must have gotten caught during a call from "Mother Nature." She always pulls a trick like that. Just then one came whistling in, and the ninety-day wonder took a lunge through a briar bush and landed head first on top of me. Luke came over to the edge of the hole and we both noticed a drop of blood or two on the lieutenant's face. I tapped ole Luke on the helmet, and at the same time asked the good lieutenant if he thought he was hit, and if so to wait till all this noise was over and then take a quick run to the aid station. As the lieutenant began to explain what he thought had happened, I tapped Luke again on the helmet and said in a very polite but sarcastic manner, "Listen to this, Mac."

"As I lunged for the hole," said the lieutenant, "the shell broke, and a fragment glazed the tip of my helmet and struck my eyebrow. Honest, I saw the spark when it glanced off the rim." With that I hit ole Luke a little harder. We want you to know that that second John got a Purple Heart the next day at the aid station. He gave them the same old song and dance, but Luke and I knew all along that a briar scratched his poor little eyebrow. What a guy won't do to get a few points!

In order to break this murder factory the Krautheads had, we would have to break out of the woods, go down the open slope fields right into the open sights and muzzles of burp guns and wire entanglements, and fight it out. It looked almost impossible, so we moved back a bit to study the situation over. Just think, a guy drawing $74.80 a month just sitting around waiting, while the mortars of Dog, How, and Mikes were giving the area a new look. They poured enough high explosives on the place to turn every tree on the place upside down. A rolling barrage, they call it.

The ugly roaring crash of 88's fell during the night as usual, but faded away at dawn while rain clouds took over. It drizzled a little, and it was cold. It was miserable! That was November 16th. The next several days were taken up with small patrol actions in the Neufmaisons area and attempts to hold on to the ground that we had fought so hard for.

We had bitter weather, as usual—rain, snow and cold—but according to the Air Corps, they could fly any time. That is, any time except the time they are most needed. We began to wonder about this very thing and were calling those fly-by-night boys damn liars. But on the 19th, things were looking up. The sun came out, so they said, and this must have been the Sunny France that everyone was talking about. Half-frozen and wet, sweating it out in those thick snow-covered woods, we couldn't half see the sun, much less feel its effects.

The Air Corps decided that today was a good day to burn up some of the taxpayers' money, and they played tag with each other while the bitter war went on below. They would swoop down in front of us and as we watched, hoping they would strafe the Jerries or find a target of some kind, they would suddenly swish up into the blue yonder. We watched hopefully, but no soap.

"It's a real comfort to know those babies are up there, but dammit-to-hell if they are going to waste gas, why in the hell can't they waste a few rounds on the Krauts. After all, it would mean a lighter load going back."

"Got a fag, Sarge?"

"Sure, here's a wet one."

About that time Rover, our best BAR man, spotted a Kraut stepping behind a tree, for only one purpose. "Hey, Sarge, watch my tracer."

With a slow, even, steady pressure on the trigger, his BAR spelled D-E-A-T-H with a five-round burst. The Heinie had just dropped his pants and was caught, literally, unfortunately. Rover's five rounds cost us four men—two dead, two wounded, for we had a little battle for about an hour after before things settled down again.

Several days had passed now, and the Nazi's defenses were slowly but surely falling apart at the seams as we moved toward the Vosges Mountains and the Alsatian Plain. It had come time for all of Uncle Sam's boys, at least those who weren't dead, to enjoy a good old Thanksgiving dinner—the Army way. Most of us were cuddled in our holes trying to keep ourselves warm from the bitter cold rain and snow, not to mention a few stray rounds kicking up the snow around the top of your hole. We hadn't given it a thought that today might have been Thanksgiving. After all, one loses all track of time when one is in the thick of fighting.

The lieutenant came over to the hole. "Tell the men if the chow jeep gets through, we will have chow after it turns dark." Never could reason with the high brass on that point. Always feed before dawn or after dark. It really didn't make that much difference to me. After all, food came first with me.

Anyway, as I proceeded to pull out of my hole to make my rounds, Jerry Boy had a dead head on me and had me zeroed in from the word go. All he was waiting for was for me to make a move. Every time I stuck my head up he would take a shot. Snipers can be contrary as hell at times, can't they? I had used the bottom of my hole several times for convenience, and I had to go again. Nothing is any better for cleaning out your foxhole than a helmet. Having cleaned my helmet out as best I could with snow and mud, I proceeded to place it in its original position on my head.

Chow finally came and was set up about three hundred yards from our holes, and scattered from one tree to another. The kitchen crew usually brought the mess kits with them, as we hadn't carried them since our first day in combat. I usually made it a practice to eat it sandwich-style between two pieces of bread or out of my hand or helmet. The mutton heads in the kitchen forgot to get the box of mess kits in the trailer before they started out. Probably too busy playing up to some French gal, whose barn they were using for a kitchen. I was determined to have Thanksgiving dinner. Nothing else to do but to take off my helmet, wash it out as best I could, and use it.

The Krautheads had us zeroed in, and just for the hell of it, dropped in a few just to let us know that they were mad because we didn't invite them for dinner. Started for the first Merry-Mac can with turkey, then potatoes, peas, cranberry sauce, buns, cake, ice cream, bread, cigarettes, candy bar and four letters from home all mixed up together in that dirty helmet with a little rain water mixed in it for good measure. I hightailed it back to my hole just in time. An 88 landed not three feet from home and added a little dirt and snow to the already pot full of chow. Must confess that it was mighty tasty and it must have been okay, for I'm still kicking and in the best of health.

As the night passed on the shelling became more intense. We lost about five dead, nine wounded, and four that had flipped their lid to the extent that they had to be held down, and taken back as Section Eights. It's rather difficult for a reader to imagine how miserable a group of men we were. For over twenty days we had existed in freezing weather, in constant snow and rain, and inconceivable danger. In all this time we had never washed or shaven. We didn't have the time. Have you ever tried to shave with ice cold water and a dull blade? Each of us expected to die at any split second, and they were carrying the wounded back to the aid station, bringing back rations and ammo. No rest. Fighting and carrying by day, fighting and carrying by night, guarding yourself and your buddies. If you were lucky you took a combat patrol out for a little party about five or six miles behind Jerry's lines.

For a general idea of how life is, just try this for size. Some stormy cold rainy January night, get out of your warm bed and go out in the back yard and with your spoon, helmet, hands, and shovel, if you are lucky enough to have one, start digging yourself a hole for protection. Every time an automobile passes by, hit the ground flat. In the meantime, get yourself a suitcase and fill it with dirt. That will in some form take the place of your pack. When you are good and wet and about half-way finished with your hole, take the suitcase and walk to the edge of town and then start cross-country for a few minutes. Don't forget to hit the ground every time you pass a car. The cars are to simulate incoming freight (artillery). Start digging another hole. When you are almost finished with it, think of that nice warm bed at home, and start on the double with suitcase in hand, hitting the ground as you pass every car. Continue this easy routine all night until dawn. Then when you approach home, give a running jump for that hole you started, which by now is full of water, and try and get some much-needed sleep. During all this maneuver one must not forget that one has a rifle which is your best friend and must be kept in working condition; one must be careful not to step on a mine, and that one is getting shot at by the enemy with one's every move.

After our heroic effort to consume our rain-soaked Thanksgiving dinner, the 399th was to move through another regiment into the attack. Leading a fatted calf to the slaughter house, I call it. The purpose of the attack was to trap a large enemy force in the middle of the Vosges Mountains between two rivers. This, the 24 November attack, left the Krautheads completely confused, and by nightfall they had lost, shall we say, their hat and ass.

While other components of the regiment were motorized, and headed for Strasbourg like a bat out of hell, we were stuck with our heads in the ground and our fannies in the air like an ostrich, at a place known to us as "The Villa." Our terrain map called it Les Quevelles. It was nothing more than a big beautiful mountainside retreat as we approached it, but later became mighty powerful. Twenty-two of the bastards finally came out after an all afternoon battle.

It was here that I had one of my closest shaves during the war. It was late afternoon and we had been under constant fire from the "Villa," with both mortar and burp-gun. The Battalion Commander had set up his CP in a farm house, in my sector, within direct sight and range of the Krautheads at the "Villa." The Commanding Officer, my ole Man, and a runner managed to get inside between mortar bursts. The runner yelled to me out of a back window, telling me that the Captain wanted me right away. The house sat about twenty-five feet from a fence, which surrounded it and had to be crossed to get to the house. I looked to the heavens for guidance and took off like a ruptured duck, hoping to make it between mortar rounds. As I crossed the fence, I heard a sudden 'swooooosh' and then a thud, which shook the ground about five feet in front of me and a little to my left. The shell itself kicked up a lot of dirt, which splattered me as I made my way to the back entrance of the house. Fortunately for me it was a dud; had it been real I would have been a post-humous receiver of the Purple Heart. No sooner had I entered the house than I saw a section of the fence blown to bits by a direct hit; the very section I had just a few seconds ago crossed.

"Killer" stayed with the bed rolls that day, because of late he had been complaining about his feet. He later went to the hospital and was sent to the States with a case of frostbite and trench foot. He was the only man in the platoon we lost due to negligence of personal hygiene. He got out of all the mess the easy way, but the men in the fighting Third went back the hard way. Fighting, drinking (when ole Luke could find it for us), digging, just plain being miserable was the agenda for the next day.

Little did we know about Bitche but we readily found out. Bitche is the "Hub" town in Alsace-Lorraine for the Maginot line.

Chapter 4

Wiped Out

ON December 5th, it was cold and snowing as usual, and we received the order to attack toward the Maginot Line. In front of us were several small towns, the Maginot Line, Bitche, then Germany and the Siegfried Line. Luke was still carrying the three EE-8As and a roll of sound-powered wire we were using for each squad, and of course a couple of bottles of Schnapps. Sometimes Schnapps, other times Cognac, but never nothing at all.

In long, haphazard files on each side of the road, battle-weary infantrymen could be seen, all dressed in different uniforms; some in raincoats, others in field jackets, all of them filthy dirty, but warm.

Alsace-Lorraine. What a place! It has been owned and operated by the Germans and the Frogs so many times that I don't believe that they really know which country they really belong to. They change hands every time the sun goes down. It's a beautiful country all right, when the sun is out. I'm afraid that they have lost their post-war tourist trade by making the GIs fight over there.

The Enchenburg, Lemberg, Mouterhouse road was the mainstay of the defenses for the Jerries, and as usual, they had it zeroed in to a "T." Mortars, machine guns and 88's were crisscrossed in a pattern that was almost impossible to cross through. During the night we could hear the rumble of armor which told us of the preparations the Krauts were making. So far, we had beaten the Krauts on their terms, and our morale was very high, considering the circumstances.

December 6th and 7th were spent trying to cross the Lemberg–Mouterhouse road by the First and Third Battalions, to no avail. Every time they would jump off, they hit a stone wall of machine gun fire and mortar fire. On December 8th the Second Battalion was called in to finish off the job if they could. Our mission was to cut off the Bitche–Lemberg Railroad and highway, thereby cutting off the city, which was to be overrun by the other two battalions.

"F" Co. took off on 8 December like a bunch of scared rabbits, and overran Suicide Hill, crossing four remaining hills thick with flak and machine gun fire which resulted in our coming to a screeching halt. After all, you can't drive a toothpick into a brick wall, can you? As dusk approached, we were still working hard on the railroad while the other battalions were trying the town out for size.

As we were ferociously digging in and fighting to hold what we already had, the Ole Man called for flank and anti-tank support, and tanks. Did we get anything? *Hell no!* During the night the first and second platoons realized the danger and every man, wounded or otherwise, remained awake all night. After all, all the Krauts had to do was to come up the trail next to the train track, in that never-to-be-forgotten flak-wagon, and wipe out the whole shootin' match.

At 0500, 9 December, the first of four hit and run flak-wagon attacks came, with his 20-mm blasting away. Rumbled right up to the foxholes. What a miserable helpless feeling that must be! Then two more attacks came off on schedule. Both of them to feel us out and each time Jerry would get a little bolder. When he saw that he was getting no return fire from anti-tank guns or tanks, which we didn't have, then came the real thing. Each time he rolled up, we tried in vain to knock him out with a bazooka.

Waller was killed at dawn the next day, along with five others trying to hit the bastard from our side of the ravine. From then on it was armor against infantry. Then came the crushing blow. There were eighty doped-up German infantrymen with 20-mm flak-wagons for support, who stormed the positions of the first and second platoons, firing point-blank into their foxholes. We were no more than fifty yards from them on our side of the ravine but had orders not to fire, until it was too late. Several of the Krauts came on our side of the track but I got two of them and someone threw a grenade and killed two, and the rest hightailed it back to where they had come from.

Several of the second platoon escaped across the track and the ravine, as the Krautheads were mad with murder. Fifty-five men were killed and captured by the Germans in less than fifteen minutes, due to the negligence of the higher muckty-mucks. Fifty-five men from an already badly depleted company left us with a handful of men, not quite a platoon. We finally managed to drive them off with the help of our flanking companies.

The Captain of "George" Company knew what had happened to "Fox" and he had to cross the same railroad. As he moved his company on, he acted as first scout. All of a sudden, the woods were full of the chatter of machine gun fire, burp-guns, and mortar bursts. Two men crawled up front to bring back the map from the dead Captain's body.

Snow flurries gave a blanket of peace over the Lemberg chaos as the entire city was cleaned out. Long files of gray-clad German uniforms marched to the rear. Our tanks took up the chase and shot up a dozen or so flak-wagons, 88's as well as a few infantry digging in. The battle for Lemberg was over, the first and most unforgettable phase of the battle for Bitche.

We tried to relax, and Luke as usual was on the prowl for something to drink. He, as he always does, found enough for all of us and we drank to those who had fallen in battle and then to Victory. After a few moments of formality and toasts, we proceeded to get tight. That is, enough to relax us and ease the tension, but not enough to keep us from doing the job that we were sent there to do.

And to think that it was the price for peace. Fifty-five men killed or captured in fifteen minutes. At the same time the Krautheads attacked, we called for a mortar concentration from "H" Company and a 4.2 outfit that was attached. At the time, this concentration of lead and steel was probably more disastrous than effective. This was the initial step in the capture of Bitche.

"Here we are going into Corps reserve after we take this town, Sarge," Luke said as he crawled into my hole with an open bottle of Schnapps. "Have a short one, it'll make you feel better."

"When do we take the place?"

"Tomorrow; it won't take long."

"Hell, man, you're off your rocker! This place is going to be the hardest to take except for Berlin. Don't you know," I said between drinks, "that Bitche has never been taken by an opposing force because of its protection and network of pillboxes?"

Bitche was located in a beautiful valley surrounded by mountains, forts and pillboxes, each of the forts and pillboxes being a separate unit with long, clear fields of fire. In the heart of this great city was a huge hill which was nothing short of an unconquerable fortress. It was like those you read about in books, built of huge gray stone, with a fifty-foot moat and draw bridges, but modern weapons. The entire network of pillboxes in the Maginot Line was connected to this great citadel by underground tunnels. These tunnels were seven to fourteen stories under the surface. They were large enough to house their own railway system, roads for trucks and bicycles, garrison troops, kitchens, warehouses and storage space for equipment and ammo. I had never dreamed of such a thing being possible. The Krauts could have locked themselves in there and stayed for years before coming out.

One of the first, Schiessick, had a disappearing hydraulic gun turret which rose to fire its huge gun, then lowered itself back into position below the surface. Hit after hit failed to knock it out. 105's, 155's, 240-mm, M12 self-propelled 155's, and finally seventy-eight fighter bombers dropped twenty-seven tons of five-hundred-pounders, about one hundred and eight bombs, before it was neutralized. The Citadel itself had a dozen or so 88's behind its gray walls, and numerous French 75's. Did someone say that it was only going to take a day? Ha! Ha! Months, Joe, months!

The French call the town Bitche, the Germans called it Bitsch, so we, the independents, called it *Bitch*. And that is exactly what it was, a bitch!

As the big picture began to take shape, our regiment had taken over the Division front. And our small band of men withdrew a thousand or so yards to Lemberg, from whence we had come. I couldn't figure it out. Only a couple of days ago we were fighting our asses off to knock the Jerries off the other side of the railroad track; now we were in the same position, waiting for the bastards to come to us.

Christmas Eve rumor had it that the Krauts were going to quit on Christmas day. Joke. Christmas day was very quiet. During the night we had moved up to an old French garrison overlooking the city of Bitche. Ole Luke and Sol had shot a rabbit and we were busy readying the hare as a dessert to our long-awaited and much talked about and overrated Christmas dinner. Jim cut down a small evergreen, which was obscuring his field of fire, and stuck it in the ground just outside the building. We proceeded to decorate the tree with ration discards, GI toilet paper, cigarettes and strands of tinfoil which the Air Force had used to jam German radar and radio nets. There was plenty to eat, smoke, and of course, ole Luke supplied us with drinks. Quiet, peace, contentment, but not for long.

Troopers jumped behind us; 11,000 men, over two hundred tanks of Hitler's crack mountain divisions were headed for Bitche. From the north, Me 109's filled the sky. German patrols began hitting their targets. Concentrations began getting heavier and heavier. A cold snowy December 31st found about 20,000 SS and mountain troops milling in and around Bitche getting primed for the kill on chocolate bars that contained dope.

"Hey Sarge, looks like the bitches in Bitche have got something brewing."

"Yeah," I said with a most puzzled look on my face.

"Yeah, probably a little New Year's Day celebration, but we are ready for them. Men are scarce up and down the line, but we'll take care of the bastards."

As the night grew darker and colder, the men grew more restless.

The clanking and clatter of tank treads in the distant produced a vivid picture of what was to happen later.

Of course, we too had a little surprise for the krauts. Every field piece on the army front had been ordered to fire on known targets at precisely 0001, 1 January 1945. Everything went according to Hoyle until the Krauts began to counterfire with all their 88's and "Screaming Meemies." By 0500 they had shot their load, and in the distance we could see gray clad figures moving to meet us. The dumb bastards hit us head on, and like a rubber ball bouncing off a brick wall, they hauled ass back where they came from. They did manage, however, to penetrate the Recon unit to our right, but after a hasty reorganization, the Recons were back in their places and the situation was back to normal.

Brown, who had been caught back at the Company CP during the attack, came running up to our CP with a canteen cup full of pink champagne and a couple of "Girlie" books.

"Al," he said as he opened the book to a picture of a nearly nude woman in a most seductive pose, "how would you like to get a real good piece of that?"

"Boy, it would only take a few minutes for me to bang that, and give her a screwing she would never forget."

"You know," he said as he lit a cigarette duck, "it's a shame for Special Service to send us this kind of stuff to look at."

"Yeah, they should send it up here in the flesh," Luke said with a chuckle.

"No kidding, though, it's good for the morale and all that sorta stuff, but it's things like that that get a guy all worked up so all he can think of is a good piece of ass. Now don't misunderstand me, there's nothing better than a good piece, but where in the hell are you going to find it up here in this God-forsaken place? Of course if we were back in the rear with all the other commandos you might be able to get a little. And if you get it, you know the Krauts have had it and you will end up with a dose. And we can't win a war in a hospital. And if a man doesn't have his mind on his work he is liable to get one through his head. No thanks, Brown, you take it."

As he turned the pages, the whistles, groans and comments were something to behold.

Again suddenly the Germans started to attack and for four long hours we fought against overwhelming odds until the Krauts decided that rather than push the fight any further, they would try to surround us. They did, but only by the fanatical impulses caused by doped-up chocolate bars. It must be one hell of a feeling for a man to know that he has to be given dope to make him fight and eventually meet death.

"Looks like we are in for it," spoke Sol in a very low sullen voice.

"In a pig's ass we are," replied Luke. "We'll get out of this mess if we have to kill every goddamn German on the front.

Why in the hell those dumb bastards at Regiment can't figure these things out is beyond me. The S-2 sits on his can all day, screws all the dames he can get at night, we do his dirty work, and he gets the medals. Wish the son-of-a-bitch would come up here and see for himself once in a while."

One could easily see that the more ole Luke talked the hotter he got.

The night was cold and dark—the only thing to break the darkness was artificial moonlight shining from the large lights in the rear echelon. I was checking the outpost when Luke tapped me on the shoulder to tell me that he thought he heard a truck coming up the road. I immediately started wondering what the hell a truck was doing up in this neck of the woods. Sure enough, the artificial moonlight silhouetted the canvas cover of a six-by-six traveling at a very slow rate of speed. Some poor joker must be lost.

As it moved slowly by the outpost, Luke yelled, "Halt—who goes there?" With this breaking the silence of the night, some Kraut took several shots at the sound, in hopes that he would scare someone. The motor was cut off, and very hurriedly the driver jumped out of the cab and rolled under the truck for protection.

Again Luke yelled, *"Halt—what's the password?"* The Germans had been known to infiltrate through and pick up jeeps, trucks, etc.—so Luke was only doing his duty. By this time there was no movement or reply from the truck. Cocking his M1, he again asked for the password. Still no answer. It was concluded that the driver was a Kraut, or a GI who had forgotten the word for the day.

"Give the pass word or I'll shoot," spoke Luke, and with this a body rolled from under the truck, in the moonlight—hands high in the air, shaking like a leaf—yelling at the top of his lungs:

"Lawd, have mercy. Don't shoot me. You know that Hitler ain't got no niggers in his Army."

With this Luke and I laughed, and told the poor fellow to jump in the hole. Having questioned him, we found that he was looking for the Company CP, which was quite some distance to the rear, and he had taken a wrong turn somewhere and had landed on the edge of no-man's-land. He was loaded with gas and ammo, and with all the noise and confusion in trying to turn the truck around, the Krauts got wise and started lobbing in a few mortars. Fortunately, the truck scampered off into darkness just as several rounds fell where it stood only a few minutes before.

That night, under the dull glow of the artificial moonlight, we saw a column of twos coming up the road toward the garrison. Dressed in GI white parka snow coats, they resembled a mass of ghosts coming to haunt the garrison. We had just received from Battalion a message stating to be on the lookout for English-speaking Germans in American uniforms who were giving a considerable amount of trouble in the rear and had been infiltrating our lines posing as GIs. Luke immediately checked with the old man to see if there were any patrols out or coming in. With a negative answer from the other end of the EE8A, he slowly pulled the lever back on the fifty-caliber gun we had set up in the window.

Having waited until the very last minute, Luke let go with a full belt. You never heard such a racket in your life. Above the loud chatter of the fifty, you could hear the bloodcurdling screams and dying groans of Hitler's supermen as they would say something in German and then slump to the ground.

The next morning Luke proudly pointed his finger through the window at the mess on the road not seventy-five yards away and said, "Goddammit, Sarge, I must have missed a couple." One mortally wounded German moved slightly and groaned in pain. He calmly picked up my carbine, took aim and slowly squeezed the trigger. As the bullet hit its mark, the body twitched and jerked as though someone were punching it with a stick.

"How the hell he lived through the night is a $64 question, Sarge."

The Krauts were hitting our lines for a bulge, but they hit in the wrong place this time. Our regiment didn't budge an inch.

It started to snow again, the hardest we'd seen so far, and the holiday setting was perfect, that is, for the folks at home. To us, only a few yards away behind a tree or bush—death waited. We shook and trembled. Not from the cold winter air but from the uncertainty of life.

"It's an awful feeling, isn't it, Luke, to be here, alive and well now, but in the next minute you may be like those bastards out there on the road."

As we sat there by the gun, snow blowing in our faces, he began to reminisce of clean clothes, a shave and a bath, a warm room and a bed, steaks, highballs, cocktails, and women. There was nothing whatsoever to do about it but to curse the bitch WAR. Hell on earth!

As the day and night passed we were prepared for another attack.

It never came off. I suppose the Krauts ran out of dope. It's a good thing, too, for even though we were ready we were still too tired and groggy to do much about it. Every division on the front was pushed back except for ours. We didn't give an inch. As the fighting simmered down a little, the night sky was streaked with blazing orange trails from "Screaming Meemies." The farm house just outside the garrison gave off a red glow as it continued to blaze through the night.

Early the next morning there was a sharp whistle on the phone. Luke, who was on guard by the gun, answered it.

"Brass hats up here—damn, they have flipped their lid haven't they?"

"O.K., I'll tell him when he wakes up. We'll get the division band, too. Yeah; O.K."

Wasn't too long before I was awakened by the sharp crack of an M1, and with a good yawn and a scratch in between the legs, I tapped Luke on the shoulder. "O.K., old man, get yourself some shut-eye."

"I can't, Sarge, just got word that the guys with the brass balls are coming up to pay their respects. We are serving tea and crumpets at 0700."

"Cut the comedy—what's on your mind?"

"Brass coming up to see us at 0700."

They were the guys who wanted you to bow and tip your helmet at the Germans before you shot them. You know—ties, clean shaves, spit and polish sorta stuff. The only way to live out here and survive is to live like a rat. And that's the way most of us lived.

As I saw the group of rear echelon commandos approaching, I proceeded to go to the basement. Ole Luke was still on the gun as the Colonel entered. Thinking that Luke was in charge, he asked, "Where is your platoon?"

Luke answered as if he were in charge. "Here, in that building, and in those holes at the base of the water tower."

"What's behind you?" asked the Colonel.

"Nothing," replied Luke.

"There is no depth in this position," said the Colonel.

"You can't have depth, sir, without men, sir," said Luke.

The Colonel cleared his throat and pointing his finger in the direction of the building across the road said, "Why, I could walk right through your positions at night."

"Yes, Sir," Luke replied as he slid down on his back a little, pushed his helmet up off his eyes a little and gave the fifty a pat on the side. "And you do, and you will be pushing up daisies like those Krauts out there who thought they could do the same thing."

The Colonel shrugged his shoulders and said, "C'mon, Captain, let's get out of here."

Everything went along pretty good for the rest of the day, that is, until about dark. I had just stepped into the building from checking the men, when I heard Luke talking on the phone.

"Okay. I'll tell him, he's out making a check."

"Who is it, Luke?"

"Ole Man wants you to take a couple of men out to the bunker, clean it out if anybody's out there, set out a couple of trip flares and get back by 2000."

"Okay. Get Sol, Brown, and Smith in here right away."

As Luke left I immediately started making plans for what was to come. As I was looking over my muddy, half-readable map, the men came in.

"Okay, fellows, we've got a job tonight."

"Shit," said Smith, "the Old Man always picks on us."

"I don't want another medal, Sarge," replied Brown.

"Shut up and listen. Sol, take a flare and some wire and get Jim's tommygun. Brown, load up with grenades and check your carbine. Smith, you get a couple of flares and wire and your tommygun. We've got a date with the bunker out in front of your squad, Smith."

"Can I go, Sarge?"

"No, Luke, you take care of the CP."

"Smith, tell your squad all about it and to cover us if anything happens. We will all meet at the water tower in five or ten minutes. Everybody know the password? If there is anything up there we will clean it out and on the way back lay the flares. We have to be back by 2000. We will break up when we near the bunker. Any questions? O.K. See you in a minute."

The boys in Smith's squad had been complaining all day about a machine gun from the bunker, so I guess it was up to us to stop it. It's a sure thing the artillery couldn't do it.

As we neared the bunker, we were about fifteen yards apart and were going to close in slowly. Everything was in dead silence. I had sent Sol towards the side door; I went straight to the aperture; Brown and Smith went to the rear. As Sol approached the door, there was a loud, sharp, German voice, "Bist du, Otto?"

"Nein," replied Sol in his best German. He lunged for the door and at the same time fired a full magazine into the bunker. Brown came running in just in time to give Sol two grenades, which exploded like the eruption of fifty field pieces. At the same time I reached into the small aperture and, much to my surprise, pulled out a burp-gun. We waited for a second, to see if all was well, then we hauled ass. Having gotten back to within a couple of hundred yards from the water tower we proceeded to lay out our flares. The next morning the burp-gun was on display at Battalion, for the benefit of some new replacements, and five dead Krauts were on display at the bunker for the benefit of the German Graves Registration.

Having been in the same positions for over two weeks, it was apparent that the winter line had been formed. With the Krauts making a breakthrough further north, there was nothing to do but to sit tight. During this time we made our holes more like home, and dug connecting trenches between holes. In a day or two we had log roofs over our holes and a network of connecting trenches that would baffle the boys at Fort Benning. Each day the men would work on their holes, fixing the tops, digging them deeper until we had a line of underground huts. Sol and Jim's hole, which was near the water tower, was large enough to sleep five men comfortably. We took great pride in our homes. It wasn't like having a room at the Astor but they were warm and cozy to a certain extent.

I suppose the big-wigs in the rear thought things were getting a little monotonous for us, so they started to shift us around. Under the cover of darkness Fox would change positions with George, and Easy with How, until each Company had hit every position, then they started moving us by Battalion. Most of us had a well-rounded "Cook's Tour" of the surrounding country side for several miles in each direction.

Van Hagan, the Company messenger, and of the Philadelphia main line, came running up and handed me a message. It gave the sign and countersign for the night, and a memo that we were to change positions with "George" beginning at 2000 with my platoon first. That's us. Always first. It began snowing again, so hard that you could hardly see your hand in front of your face. At about 1945 I had gotten the platoon together and started to move out when I remembered that I had forgotten the sound-powered phone which was still in the CP hole.

I returned to retrieve it and, much to my surprise, I found in the bottom of the hole, a stinking, dirty, filthy Kraut. The machine guns were having a party that night, and he evidently took refuge in the hole I had just vacated. As I stood over the hole with my rifle pointed at his head, he slowly rose with the "hande hoch" and was giving out with the same old stuff. "Kamerad. Nix geschossen." I could have let him have it then and there, but thought it rather amusing that such a thing should happen at a time like this.

"Rouse, you bastard!"

The platoon proceeded to move out to make the exchange with "George," first stopping at the Company CP to drop off our newly acquired rifleman.

February 1st was an unusual day for us, especially that night. The outpost of Conn's squad was particularly on the ball that night and there had been several little fights off and on during the night.

As I peered into the blackness of the sky I heard a faint whistle and cry over the sound-powered.

"Tiger 1 calling Fox 3. Tiger 1 calling Fox 3."

"Hey, Sarge, Sarge,"—then a faint whistle again and again, and another "Hey Sarge."

As I picked up the receiver, I spoke very quietly.

"Okay. Tiger 1, what d'you want? This is Fox 3."

"Hey Sarge, this outpost hotel not only has hot and cold running bullets, but they serve you hot and cold running dames."

"Cut the comedy, what's up?"

"We got a gal, coming up the road into the garrison about fifteen minutes ago. What do you want to do with her?"

"Bring her back to the CP."

In a few minutes we heard them coming through the woods and in a few seconds they jumped into the trench that led to the opening to the CP hole.

"Hey, look at this. Not bad. Not bad at all. Boy, look at those boobies," said 'Mousey,' as he gently reached over and fondled her breast. She didn't seem to mind, at least she didn't make any attempt to stop him. Ha ... What difference did it make? If she had tried to stop him he would have roughed her up a little bit. So what's the difference?

"Did all of you take a crack at her? She looks all beat."

"Naw, Sarge, she ain't clean looking and you know what the posters back home say about VD."

We debated for a few minutes as to the proper interrogating procedure in a case like this, asked her a few questions to no avail, kicked her in the butt, and sent her to the rear, with ole Luke as her congenial escort.

And so it was, all winter long in those goddamned foxholes. Morale was slacking and spasmodic. Being in the woods in a hole during the cold rain and snow season would, I suppose, have a lot to do with the morale of troops.

Morale—what is morale? Can you touch it? See it? Morale is a Company Jeep pulling up a muddy, sloppy trail with chow or PX supplies and men in a foxhole wondering which one will be the eight-ball to screw up the works. Morale is drawing names for passes to Paris or Brussels. Three days—long enough to forget the horrors of war. Morale is standing guard from eight to ten, or two to four—most of all, morale is knowing that you are going into Reserve.

February 9th, the 100th consecutive day in combat, was gloriously celebrated by diving, spitting American Thunderbolts, piloted by German aviators. What a life! And no sign of an ending. They played hell with us all day. You could hardly stick your head out of your hole. Our little angels of the wild blue yonder couldn't fly that day; they had a hangover or something. If the Germans could fly, so could our boys, but there was no interruption and the bastards with the black cross had a field day.

As the darkness of night closed in, artificial light bounced off of low hanging clouds to afford more light for our OP's and to direct night artillery.

Cold rains on the 12th melted the snow on the hills and the German high muckity-mucks were beginning to make a change in their troops. The Volksgrenadier troops were relieved by the German 2nd Mountain Div., which was relieved several days later by the crack 6th SS Mountain Division. Old man Hitler was placing his crack experienced SS mountain troops to fight in the hills around that all-important city of Bitche. Bed-check Charlie, the last of the Luftwaffe, made his usual rounds taking pictures. He flew so high that you could hardly hear him.

By March 7th, replacements started arriving to build up our badly depleted ranks. New faces, inexperienced eight-balls, rumors. Psychological warfare began to play its part.

A 4F Goes to War

Early morning of March 8th found Luke hitting me with his fist.

Sarge, there's a jeep coming up the road from the rear. The guy must be lost."

As the jeep closed in a voice over the phone said: "Guys from Signal Company and G-2 section coming up in your area.

"Okay."

As the jeep pulled up a very small anemic 2nd John hopped out, and scaring him half to death, I called through the window. "What'cha got, Lieutenant?"

"We're going to set up this loudspeaker by the window and talk to the Jerries down the road."

"You had better get that damn jeep around the side of the house before the Krauts decide it's time for target practice with their mortars."

His driver was very careless and noisy and as a result the Krauts decided to throw in a couple of practice rounds. The lieutenant and his driver both took off for the basement like a pair of scared rabbits. Luke and I laughed like hell.

"Is everything okay, Sarge?" asked the lieutenant as he peered around the basement door.

"Yeah."

"What's the matter with you guys? Suppose we took off for the basement every time they threw in a couple, who would man the gun to keep them from coming up the road? Let's get it right, Lieutenant, maybe you've been behind a desk too long."

"That's enough out of you, Sarge."

"Yes, Sir," I replied laughingly, as I punched Luke in the side.

"Yeah," said Luke, "you go right ahead with your work, don't let us bother you."

In about half an hour after everything was set up, they started playing a record, and its translation went something like this: "Come, comrades, give up. Come alone or in groups of two's.

Make your way to open ground and follow the road west to the American lines. Stay in the open with your hands high, palms out, and no weapons. Don't try to climb the hills or go into the woods or you will be sorry. Go west, young man, go west."

They played that damn thing over and over again until I was sick and tired of hearing it. I felt like letting a few rounds go right into the loudspeaker.

"Hey, Sarge, what they gonna do—talk 'em out rather than shoot 'em out? Sounds good to me. It's the safest way. Why didn't they start fighting a war this way in the beginning?"

"Krauts," shouted Luke as he pulled the cocking lever back on the fifty caliber.

A column of two's—hands high, all carrying a white hankie—marching in step as though they were followed by a band. Thirty-eight of them, and they said that there were more—about fifty—who wanted to come but their superiors threatened to kill them if they left. Poor guys—probably got shot anyway.

Old man Sun put in long hours on March 14th, and the sky overhead was filled with P-47s and P-51s bombing and strafing German rear echelons and Bitche. Several squadrons of Flying Forts passed over with their sights on Bitche. She was in for a terrific pounding and got it. All day long. It was like having a grandstand seat at an air show. Thrilling sight, but in our hearts we knew that all the fuss was not in fun. It was just a softening up for what was to come later.

That night we were relieved to go back several hundred yards to get our attack orders. With the fighting third platoon in the lead, on March the 15th, we started our own private war on the proud citadel, one day before the Seventh Army jump-off.

Chapter 5

Bitche

A T 0600 on March 15th, the third platoon led the attack on Bitche in our sector after a tremendous artillery barrage. With three tanks attached, we moved cautiously and slowly. Some men were on top of the tanks crouched behind the turret and others followed to the rear of the tanks. There was a considerable amount of wire and mines, and it was the purpose of the tanks to make an opening in the wire and to explode the mines. The Germans had over two months to prepare their positions and we knew that it wasn't going to be easy. It would have been the same if the shoe were on the other foot.

As I crouched behind the lead tank, I grasped for the telephone mounted on the back, and in a low and shaky voice, gave "O.K. Let's go," to the tank commander. The noise of the tank was terrific and obviously drew very much unwanted artillery and small arms fire from the already-awakened Wehrmacht.

"Follow closely in the track of the tank treads," I cautioned all. There were possibly four thousand shu-mines in the area, and I didn't want anyone going home with one leg. After moving about twenty-five yards from our initial jump-off, our tank threw a tread.

"Goddammit, of all the fucking luck," was the sentiment of every man. What a spot. In no-man's-land behind a tank that won't run and not able to move because of the mines.

"Don't step off the tracks," I yelled. At that second a decision had to be made. I signaled for the second tank to move up, and at the same time I shouted instructions through the telephone to the most impatient commander inside. As the second tank rumbled closer I had the most unforgettable feeling that something drastic was going to happen.

And it did. Just as the second tank was pulling up alongside the lead tank, and Sol, "Todo," and "Joe Stalin" had leaped to take refuge on top of the second tank, an '88' hit about two feet from the right side. It blew Sol sprawling but unhurt to the ground at the rear of the tank. "Todo" and "Joe Stalin" were less fortunate, however, in that they were mortally wounded. "Todo" hit the ground on his back smack on top of a mine, and "Joe Stalin" was hanging limply over the side of the tank with blood gushing from his neck.

We moved slowly towards the Kraut position, which made their machine gun and small arms fire more effective.

"Medic," a loud yell pierced the noise of battle. Bass had gotten a burp-gun through the leg. As the gray smoke of burned gun powder and the gloom of early morning cleared, we began to orient ourselves more definitely. When we had passed a mined area, we began to spread out and give the Jerries a taste of their own medicine.

During the onslaught of battle, I happened to survey the two knocked-out tanks behind me. They had fired up all of their ammo and the men were coming through the hatches as fast as you ever saw. They started running the minute they hit the ground. I don't suppose they stopped running until they reached the Battalion CP. Two of them didn't make it because of mines. Need I say more?

As the battle became more intense, Sergeant Bazzo of the weapons platoon picked up his light machine gun off its mount, threw the ammo belt across his shoulder, and waded into the German position, neutralizing two burp-guns, killing six Krauts and capturing fourteen. By mid-morning we had broken through and began to advance. By now three of our tanks had been knocked out and a fourth was pressing the attack. By 1200 we had slugged our way to the tip of Spitzberg Ridge, a distance of a little over 1,000 yards. It's a slow, endless, hard war.

The second day of the attack saw a complete reduction of the proud city of Bitche, the citadel of the Maginot Line. According to the *Stars and Stripes*, Bitche was taken with hardly a shot. Well, every man has a right to his own opinion.

"Hey, Sarge. How come we fight our asses off for four cold long months and then we march through it and out the other side in ten minutes?"

"Das ist der Krieg."

As the Krauts withdrew and we pushed onward, they fought not even a delaying action, mostly sniper fire here and there. Of course this was also dangerous, that is, if you were the figure to cross the hairline on their telescopic sights.

On 17 March, at about 1430, the so-called "Sons of Bitche" cautiously walked passed the stone marker on the border to lead us to the land of the "Supermen." Gleaming on the distant hillside lay the ugly dragon teeth of the Siegfried Line. With a screeching halt we proceeded to digging. Platoons in Germany, platoon CPs in France. Would it ever end?

Chapter 6

Heilbronn

THE second day of spring found us loaded on everything and anything that had four wheels—trucks, jeeps, tanks, half-tracks, and captured German vehicles. Objective Mannheim. Civilians and white flags hung from the windows getting their first look at their conquerors. They saw sand-bagged Shermans and battle-worn soldiers, human hand grenade trees, camouflaged helmets, ripped jackets, bearded faces, "Space Cadet" goggles weary from endless days of fighting.

Occasionally a daring Me 110 would strafe, but nothing serious happened as we rolled along through a land of red and white villages only a few kilometers apart. Roadside littered with knocked-out vehicles of both sides. Thirty kilometers to Mannheim, then twenty, then ten, then seven. March 24th gave us our first sight of the Rhine. The famed Rhine. Humph!

As we prepared our positions, we kept a watch on factories and cranes still at work turning out war material across the river. Sniper fire and 88's were the order of the day, and it kept us quite entertained.

"This is the way to fight a war," laughed ole Luke as he emerged from a basement with an arm load of Schnapps and champagne. "I hate to take all this, but you know how it is, Sarge, I'm thirsty."

"Sure, what are you going to do with it?"

"There's more down there, we'll dish it out to the platoon to kick the Jerries out of their houses." We celebrated. For the war was almost over, we thought. Schnapps for all. A good night's rest with soft music furnished by the whistling 88's.

On 31 March, with the help of overcast skies, we crossed the symbolic river at a distance of about 300 yards. Crossing from Ludwigshaffen into the now well-flattened Mannheim, we fanned out and turned south parallel to the river to greet the on-coming French Second Corps. We were now moving at a pretty fast pace and the first week in April was spent taking several small towns between Mannheim and Heilbronn.

On 5 April we were to cross the Neckar River. Our small and flimsy beachhead consisted of a factory and a couple of houses along the river bank. Don't think for a minute that it was a picnic. Taking a boat ride across the Neckar is like striking a match to a barrel of gun powder. Broad open daylight, no smoke screen and the hills beyond full of 88's. We managed to make the landing, but not for long.

On 7 April the Krauts threw in a counterattack with four King Tiger tanks and many men. They managed to push hell out of some units, moving them all the way back to the river bank. The battle for Heilbronn was on, and from the looks of things it was going to be a dilly. Heilbronn was the biggest battle in the world on 7 April, yet not a single man was visible. That's what battle is.

"Here come the Meemies," someone shouted, and even the fellows in the cellars, taking a drink or playing up to some gal, tried to crawl under something. The sky was full of fireworks: 88's, Meemies, mortars, and SP-76's. As a result the Engineers could not give us a permanent crossing. Every time they would get it completed the Krauts would blow it up.

War, platoon by platoon, squad by squad, man by man, hit and run, run and hit, factory to factory, house to house, room to room, over dead Krauts, through rubbish, under barbed wire, over fences, in the windows and out the doors, sweating, cussing, firing, throwing grenades, charging into blazing houses, shooting through floors and closet doors—thirty seconds for a puff on a cigarette—fighting—War!

The battle for Heilbronn was a battle of supply boats, communications, attacks and counterattacks, house to house fighting, Panzerfaust teams, automatic weapons, snipers, Meemies, King Tigers, and the damned little Hitler Jugend.

"It's taking us a long time to clean up this baby, and we ain't through yet," remarked Luke. "Where in the hell are all the bastards coming from? We've killed enough to supply an army and they are still coming and still shooting."

At twilight on the 12th, we headed south down the road along the river bank toward Sontheim, as usual the third platoon in the lead. As we neared the outskirts of the town, all hell broke loose. To our left front was a large white house with an orchard from which they could spot our every move. With the first crack of the rifle, we hit the sides of the road and took up the firefight. All squads deployed to the left of the road with the exception of the bazooka team and the BAR which were hidden by the bank of the river on the right. We blasted away, and in about one and one-half hours we managed to move into town and take over an old factory building.

I don't know what kind of factory it was, as we didn't have time to call on the manager and go on an escorted inspection tour. As the darkness of night descended upon us, artificial moonlight came on and the artillery concentrated on targets in the German half of Sontheim. We nestled in windows and doorways for the night and between artillery bursts listened for the sound of hobnailed shoes. That night was a frightful one, as were many others, in that we entered the town at night and were not properly oriented as to the exact position of the Krauts. Maybe they were around the corner, or even in the next room.

As dawn broke the next morning, we moved out. One by one from his shelter, and in a very few minutes we knew where the Krauts were. All around us. We took up the firefight and started moving ahead, over fences, through houses, up back alleys, over coal piles and debris. It became more like fun, a game, than it did a war. I had lost contact with the squads for the time being, but I was confident that they were moving as fast as they could when they could. In the distance I could hear Conn shouting to his men or yelling something in German.

Momentarily there was a slight lull in the business, and with carbine in hand and Luke following behind, we approached an alley in front of us, running from our left straight down to the river.

"Hey, Sarge, let's slow down a little."

"Okay. Let's have a smoke."

"Get behind that chicken coop."

"Where is Sol?" I asked.

"He said that he was going to follow Conn's squad."

We took a couple of drags off our cigarettes and doubled across the yard into the back door of the house. We checked the house quickly to see if anyone was there, Luke going upstairs and I took off for the basement.

"Find anything?"

"Nothing yet."

As I reached the bottom of the basement steps I heard someone speaking German and groaning. I waited for Luke to come down, and as he kicked the door open I yelled "Hande Hoch." Much to my amazement, there was "Jazbo" getting a good piece of ass from a very attractive fraulein.

"I heard your voice when you came in, Sarge, so I knew that it wasn't the Krauts. I dropped down here to get a bit of much-needed rest, and this is what I find. Not bad, eh? All I said was 'Hello,' and she lay back on these bags of potatoes. What would you have done, Sarge?"

We paid no attention whatsoever to "Jazbo's" extra activities (nor did they to us) and after a ten minute rest in this den of iniquity, we went topside to see how the war was progressing.

Standing in the doorway, I decided to make a dash across the back yard to the alley. As I ran out of the yard into the alley, much to my surprise the whole damned thing was covered by burp guns and they all opened up. I dodged and shifted until I had made my way into the doorway of a house across the alley where I very nervously caught a breather. I was certain that this was the end for me. I had the feeling that the Krauts had their sights set for me today. So far I had been lucky, but this was getting a little too close for comfort. Standing in the doorway, I realized that I was a clay pigeon for anyone wanting to take a shot at me from a window.

I stepped out of the doorway, head down, and in a low crouched position broke into a very tired but slow run. The Lord must have been with me, for at that instant I looked up, and in front of me, not more than fifty feet away, were two Germans with rifles. They fired, and at the same time I fired eight fast rounds from my hip, spun to the right about and hauled ass back across the alley. The burp-gun opened up at me again. In the course of my informal meeting with the two Germans, I had completely forgotten about the burp-guns. I was really scared.

With that extra stock of energy that only God gives in time of crisis, I ran down the alley to the corner and around it doing eighty, and ran smack into an abandoned trolley. Diving, as though I were going swimming, into the door and on the floor, out of breath and tired, I decided to take a short rest, occasionally peeping over the windows to make sure that a couple of Jerries weren't following me.

Lying on the floor, I could hear the familiar zing of machine gun bullets passing overhead, and to the rear the unforgettable sound of tanks. My first thought was, whose tank? As I crawled to the rear of the trolley, bullets continued to break all the glass and shatter the sides. I wondered just why an American would be shooting up the works behind our troops. The French, it's understandable. Maybe the Germans are coming in from the rear. His guns had ceased and I slowly peeped out the back window. It was an American tank. Cautiously I took my handkerchief from my pocket, and waved it through the already shattered window. I slowly stepped from the back door of the trolley in full view of the oncoming tank. With arms outstretched, I signaled for him to come up. Seeing that I was a GI, he threw the tank into high gear and sped toward me. As the tank approached I noticed the driver's hatch opening up, and the Joe driving spoke loudly:

"What in the hell are you doing up this far?"

"That's a damn stupid remark to make, what do you think I'm doing, making a speech?"

"I just wondered, you're about four blocks ahead of everybody else."

Bang—I realized that I had been in no-man's land. I gave a loud yell for Luke and "Jazbo," but no answer. I suppose they went back to the basement for more morale.

I hopped upon the tank, the driver shoved her into reverse, and we backtracked for four blocks. It wasn't until I dismounted from the tank that I noticed that the stock of my carbine had been nicked three times, evidently by the two Krauts in the alley. The rest of the day was spent in hot combat, pushing ahead, cleaning out the town.

Friday, the 13th, was a lucky day for us rather than unlucky. Many decorations were won, the SS troops and Grenadiers were not scared troops anxious to surrender, but they were outbattled. The capture of Sontheim marked the bitter end of the nine-day struggle for Heilbronn.

A 4F GOES TO WAR

Chapter 7

Surrender

SPRING was in the air, and there was no rest for the weary, for we were chasing Jerry on the rough roads to the south. As we moved swiftly, the greenery of the rolling hills loomed in front of us. Speed was essential; the enemy must be caught, surrendered and annihilated. To let him escape means to fight him another day. In moving so rapidly southward, attempting to climb some of those everlasting hills proved to be one of the costliest efforts made by our unit. To the ever present and terrifying Kraut mortar fire, they had added a dual concentration of artillery and small arms fire. It seemed then that there was no getting away from it.

A little further south, Talheim had been prepared for us with many machine guns, backed up with those coughing mortars—it was a bitter and bloody battle all the way, but as the attack began to get into full swing, the Krauts began to give in.

Fox Company and the fighting third patrolled the town of Talheim to find that the French had all under control, so we were ordered to the higher ground near Lauffen—where the same old seven and six took place. Well, there was one helluva battle. Jerry's 88's and 120's started falling, each one with a number on it and each one with a target; 18 April was one of the costliest days of the whole damn war. Most of those left who had been at Anzio say that it exceeded all they had experienced in Italy. Shells coming in by the hundreds; hundreds of screaming, groaning hysterical voices calling for a Medic—but there weren't enough pill-rollers to go around. The attack went on, and to add to the agony and confusion, Jerry decided to counterattack.

"Look, Sarge, must be fifty or sixty of the bastards," said Luke, with an air of fright in his eyes.

"Let 'em have it," I yelled. I was scared. No matter how long you have been on the line, no matter how many counterattacks you have faced, no matter how well you are prepared for it, and no matter how hard you pray, no matter how brave, you are still scared. Don't let anyone tell you different. About an hour later, after resorting to every available weapon, including pistols, Jerry gave up—thank goodness.

The days were getting warmer and more pleasant, the skies were clear and blue, and we, along with hundreds of others, had cracked the Kraut line east of the Neckar river. We had opened the gates to the south to Stuttgart, Munich and the Brenner Pass.

Playing greyhound-catch-the-rabbit with Jerry was becoming great fun for us until 20 April when we had another beauty outside of Backnang which lasted most of the afternoon. The Engineers quickly threw a bridge across the Murr River for us and the race was on again. During this little party, we had managed to cut off 270 square miles of German troops between the snaking Neckar River and Backnang.

April 22nd was "Tinker's" day with his first squad going into Rotenberg and capturing over one hundred prisoners—this was the clincher. We had a feeling that all was lost for Jerry. On 25 April we were pulled out of the line and put into reserve after 175 consecutive days of hell. In 185 days of combat operations the fighting third platoon lost three lieutenants and thirty-eight men. Only five of the original platoon returned.

On 2 May, while we were still trying to catch Jerry, and after leading the fighting third platoon most of the way from November 1944, I was proud to receive a Battlefield Commission. I suppose they had scraped the bottom of the barrel and had no one else to choose from. I had been leading the 3rd Platoon for approximately six months with no officer. Nevertheless, in the few minutes it took for the ceremony, I was given bars, signed papers, discharged as an enlisted man and sworn in as an officer, shook hands with the General and within a couple of hours was back on top of a tank chasing Jerry.

We had been moving fast, mostly on tanks, fighting all the way. It was evident that the Nazi machine was near total collapse. It was at first a matter of days, then hours. On 8 May, with a sign of "Strike" and a countersign of "One," the good news came of surrender. Some of us took a last shot at a fleeing Kraut, others shook hands; Luke and I hugged each other with joy, and others got slopped-up on Schnapps. We had come a long way since we first met Jerry in his own backyard. We had battled the Vosges Mountains, something never before accomplished in military history, and liberated Bitche, the French fortress which had never fallen to an invading army in over two hundred years.

So ended the bloody business of the day, and how wonderful it would have been if the dead could have drunk with us in victory.

Chapter 8

Aftermath

ON 10 or 11 May we were billeted outside the city of Ulm, and received a message to go to the marshaling yards in Ulm to round up German soldiers who would not surrender. We took a jeep and trailer with a .50 caliber machine gun mounted, extra ammunition, grenades, and a bullhorn. They were armed to the hilt and had not gotten the word that the war was over. As soon as we made our cautious approach all hell broke loose. We had one helluva firefight for about three hours before we could convince them to come out with "Hande hoch." Fortunately, no one was hurt, but here I am still fighting three days after the cease fire.

In July 1945 I was assigned as DP train commander to take a load of DPs to the Russian border. I had six enlisted men including a cook. There were rations, a stove, and a truck and gas strapped to a flat car and, along with the Russian officer and his men, we took off. I do not remember the town, but I remember it took about five to six days to get there and three days to get back to Stuttgart.

In August 1945 I was ordered to go to Stuttgart to play football for the 100th Division, as I had played at Duke University before going into the service.

In January 1946 I received some R&R in Switzerland for seven days at Davos. I returned to my unit in Phorzheim and was immediately sent to Bremerhaven to join an Army amphibious battalion for home. There I got stuck on the ship *Sadalia Victory* in the harbor for two weeks because of a maritime union strike.

In March 1946 I was separated from the Army at Fort George Meade, Maryland. I went to Durham, North Carolina, where I immediately started to work in a tobacco factory one day after arriving. I remained in the tobacco or related business for forty years before retiring.

The Author

JOHN C. Angier III was born in 1922. After attempting to enlist in the Navy, who turned him down due to his being color blind and short-sighted, he enlisted in the Army in October 1942 and entered the service on 19 November 1942 at Fort Bragg, North Carolina. While serving overseas he received word from his Draft Board that he had been classified as "4F" due to his being color blind and short-sighted, as well as having flat feet and a spur-like growth under both feet. He served with the original 501st Parachute Battalion, trained with the 2nd Ranger Battalion and spent the rest of his active duty with the 100th Infantry Division.

John was promoted from Private to PFC on 19 January 1943, to Corporal on 20 March 1943, to Sergeant on 26 April 1943, to Staff Sergeant on 7 September 1943, to Technical Sergeant on 2 February 1944, and received a Battlefield Commission to Second Lieutenant on 2 May 1945 at Bad Constadt, Germany.

Separated from the service at Fort Meade, Maryland, on 28 March 1946. Promoted to First Lieutenant in the North Carolina National Guard on 11 February 1949 and in the National Guard on 23 March 1949. Honorably discharged as a First Lieutenant, Infantry, National Guard, on 11 September 1951. He served twelve and a half years in the North Carolina National Guard and the Virginia State Guard. Retired as a Major in 1958.

During his tenure in the service he received thirteen decorations including the Combat Infantry Badge, Bronze Star with Cluster, Good Conduct, Victory Medal, Occupation Germany Medal, Expert Infantry Badge, American Defense Medal and National Security Medal. He fought in three campaigns: Southern France, Alsace, and Germany.

John is widowed and currently living in St. Augustine, Florida, where he is a member of American Legion Post #37 and a life member of VFW Post #2391. He is serving his fifth term as National Adjutant for the National Order of Battlefield Commissions. John has three children: John, Charlotte and Charles.

Documents
Maps
Photographs

HEADQUARTERS SEVENTH ARMY

APO 758   US ARMY

2 May 1945

SUBJECT : APPOINTMENT

TO   :   2d Lt John C. Angier, III, 02 014 954
              399th Infantry Regiment
              APO 447, U S Army

    1. The Secretary of War has directed that you be informed that the President has appointed and commissioned you a temporary second lieutenant in the Army of the United States effective **2 May 1945.**
This appointment may be vacated at any time by the President and, unless sooner terminated, is for the duration of the present emergency and six months thereafter. Your serial number is **02 014 954.**

    2. This letter should be retained by you as evidence of your appointment as no commissions will be issued during the war.

BY COMMAND OF LIEUTENANT GENERAL PATCH :

W. G. CALDWELL
Colonel, AGD
Adjutant General

R E S T R I C T E D

HEADQUARTERS SEVENTH ARMY
APO 758   US Army

SPECIAL ORDERS)   7 May 1945
            :
NUMBER   127)   E X T R A C T

**   **   **

18. VOCG ordering ea of the fol named O, AUS to FAD, DP, eff dates indicated, and asgmt as indicated, are made of record, the urgency having been
such as to prevent the issuance of orders in advance. FDCMR: Same as date
of rank. Auth: Cir No 10, Hq European T of Opns, dtd 27 Jan 45.

NAME	PRES STA AND ASGMT	EFF DATE W/RANK FR	DUTY WITH
**	**		**
2D LT RICHARD C. YARDLEY 02 014 978	398th Inf Regt APO 447	4 May 45	Inf
2D LT JOHN C. ANGULP, III 02 014 954	399th Inf Regt APO 447	2 May 45	Inf
2D LT ROY N. FULL 02 014 952	399th Inf Regt APO 447	2 May 45	Inf
2D LT THOMAS F. WORSHAM 02 014 957	399th Inf Regt APO 447	2 May 45	Inf
2D LT JULIUS DEL MESE 02 014 955	399th Inf Regt APO 447	2 May 45	Inf
2D LT LOUIS F. LEVY 02 014 958	399th Inf Regt APO 447	2 May 45	Inf
2D LT LIBERATO DI BATTISTA 02 014 951	399th Inf Regt APO 447	2 May 45	Inf
2D LT WILLIAM C. HUFF 02 014 955	399th Inf Regt APO 447	2 May 45	Inf
**	**		**

BY COMMAND OF LIEUTENANT GENERAL PATCH:

                                        ARTHUR A. WHITE
                                        Major General, GSC
OFFICIAL: Chief of Staff

        s/ W. G. Caldwell (k)
        t/ W. G. CALDWELL
           Colonel, AGD
           Adjutant General

A TRUE COPY: R E S T R I C T E D

        JACOB NOBUT
        CRO 399th Inf
        Asst Pers O

R E S T R I C T E D

HEADQUARTERS 100TH INFANTRY DIVISION
Office of the Commanding General
APO 447, U.S. Army

AG 300.4   29 July 1945

SUBJECT: Orders.

TO   : See Distribution.

1. The following Officer and Enlisted Men, 399th Infantry, are placed
on temporary duty with Displaced Personnel Teams and will report on this
date to Major Boon, Displaced Persons Commander, at 2A Rotestrasse, Stuttgart,
Germany, for instructions:

                    2D LT JOHN C ANGIER III 02014954 INF
                    S Sgt Francis R Tomlinson 39001112
                    S Sgt James A Primavera 31736038
                    Tec 5 Roy T Vann 20811569
                    Tec 5 Arthur J Huston Jr 32655801
                    Tec 5 Lemuel B Cole 34515715 (Driver)
                    Pfc Joseph J Hurley Jr 31360840

2. Officer and Enlisted Men will take blankets and rations for four (4)
days. One three-quarters ton truck will be used. Upon completion of temporary
duty, Officer and Enlisted Men will return to their proper organization and
station. The travel directed is necessary in the military service. (Authority:
Ltr Hq VI Corps, file AG 210.453, Sub: Pers for DP Teams, dated 16 Jul 45)

                    BY COMMAND OF MAJOR GENERAL BURRESS:

                                                    BYRON C DE LA MATER
                                                    Lt Col AGD
                                                    Adjutant General

DISTRIBUTION
2 - Lt Angier III
1 - 399th Inf
1 - Hq XXI Corps
1 - AG File
1 - Returns
1 - SO Sec

R E S T R I C T E D

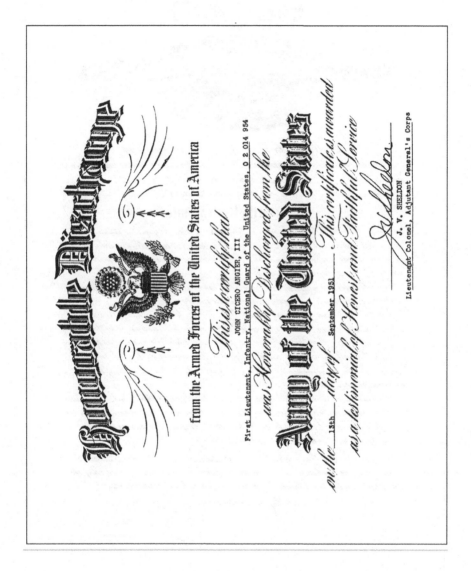

Honorable Discharge

from the Armed Forces of the United States of America

This is to certify that

JOHN CICERO ANGIER, III

First Lieutenant, Infantry, National Guard of the United States, O 2 014 954

was Honorably Discharged from the

Army of the United States

on the 13th day of September 1951   This certificate is awarded

as a testimonial of Honest and Faithful Service

J. V. SHELDON
Lieutenant Colonel, Adjutant General's Corps

THE
PRESIDENT
OF
THE UNITED STATES OF AMERICA

To all who shall see these presents, greeting:

Know Ye, that reposing special trust and confidence in the patriotism, valor, fidelity and abilities of   John Cicero Angier

I do appoint him   Second Lieutenant, Infantry   *in the*

Army of the United States

such appointment to date from the   twenty-eighth   *day of*   March *nineteen hundred and*   forty-six   *He is therefore carefully and diligently to discharge the duty of the office to which he is appointed by doing and performing all manner of things thereunto belonging.*

He will enter upon active duty under this commission only when specifically ordered to such active duty by competent authority.

And I do strictly charge and require all Officers and Soldiers under his command when he shall be employed on active duty, to be obedient to his orders as an officer of his grade and position. And he is to observe and follow such orders and directions, from time to time, as he shall receive from me, or the future President of the United States of America, or the General or other Superior Officers set over him, according to the rules and discipline of War.

This Commission evidences an appointment in the Army of the United States, under the provisions of section 37, National Defense Act, as amended, and is to continue in force for a period of five years from the date above specified, and during the pleasure of the President of the United States, for the time being.

Done at the City of Washington, this   nineteenth   *day of*   December *in the year of our Lord one thousand nine hundred and*   forty-six , *and of the Independence of the United States of America the one hundred and*   seventy-first

By the President:

Adjutant General.

W. D., A. G. O. FORM No. 0650 C.
AUGUST 1, 1938

THE PRESIDENT OF THE UNITED STATES OF AMERICA

To all who shall see these presents, greeting:

Know Ye, that reposing special trust and confidence in the patriotism, valor, fidelity and abilities of _____ John Cicero Angier, Third _____,

I do appoint him _____ First Lieutenant, Infantry _____,

National Guard of the United States in
The Army of the United States

such appointment to date from the _____ twenty-third _____ day of _____ March _____, nineteen hundred and _____ forty-nine _____. He is therefore carefully and diligently to discharge the duty of the office to which he is appointed by doing and performing all manner of things thereunto belonging.

He will enter upon active duty under this commission only when ordered to such active duty by competent authority.

And I do strictly charge and require all Officers and Soldiers under his command when he shall be employed on active duty to be obedient to his orders as an officer of his grade and position. And he is to observe and follow such orders and directions from time to time, as he shall receive from me, or the future President of the United States of America, or the General or other Superior Officers set over him, according to the rules and discipline of War.

This Commission to continue in force during the pleasure of the President of the United States, for the time being.

Done at the City of Washington, this _____ twentieth _____ day of _____ May _____, in the year of our Lord one thousand nine hundred and _____ forty-nine _____, and of the Independence of the United States of America, the one hundred and _____ seventy-third _____.

By the President:

(signature)
Adjutant General.

W. D., A. G. O. FORM No. 0652 B.
JULY 1, 1936

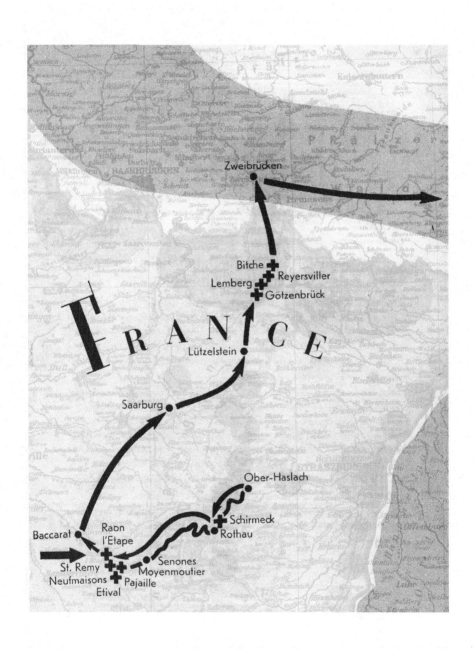

Zweibrücken

Bitche
Reyersviller
Lemberg
Götzenbrück

Lützelstein

Ober-Haslach

Saarburg

Schirmeck
Rothau

Baccarat
Raon
l'Etape
Senones
Moyenmoutier
St. Remy
Neufmaisons   Pajaille
Etival

FRANCE

94

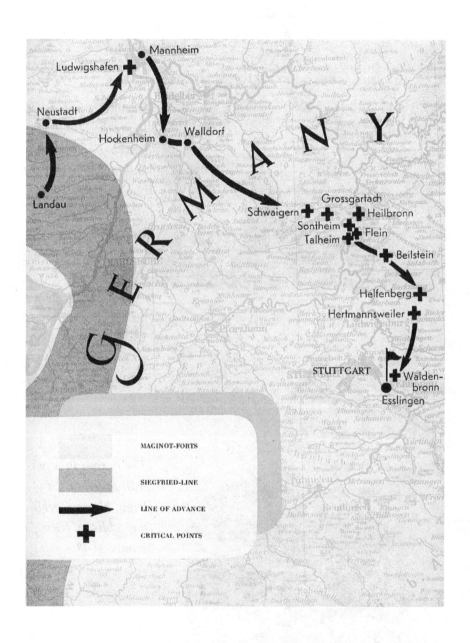

Mannheim

Ludwigshafen ✚

Neustadt

Hockenheim ● Walldorf

Landau

G E R M A N Y

Schwaigern ✚ ✚   Grossgartach
         Sontheim ✚ ✚ Heilbronn
         Talheim ✚✚ Flein
                   ✚ Beilstein

                   Helfenberg ✚

                   Hertmannsweiler ✚

         STUTTGART   ✚ Wälden-
                              bronn
                   Esslingen

MAGINOT-FORTS

SIEGFRIED-LINE

LINE OF ADVANCE

✚ CRITICAL POINTS

The author at Camp Toccoa, Georgia, 501st Parachute Infantry Regiment, December 1942. He had to wait for boots and fatigues—he had blue fatigues while all the others got green.

The author in a portrait taken in Raleigh, North Carolina, while on leave, winter 1943.

The author was an instructor in the "Nazi Village," where they used live ammo. All men were from different units of the 100th Division, forming an experimental company. The author is third from the right (the first figure is barely visible in the shadows) in the darker-colored (blue) fatigues. On his left is Sgt. Bull of the 399th Inf. Regt., the first to receive the Expert Infantryman's Badge in the U.S. Army. The author was fifty-third out of two hundred. Fort Jackson, summer 1943.

The author's "Nazi village," built especially to be taken by "trainees," using ball ammunition, in street fighting from house to house.

The author, left end of middle row, with glasses. Fort Bragg, summer 1944.

Shoulder patch of the 100th Infantry Division. The numeral "100" is half white (upper) and half yellow (lower) on a deep blue shield.

Early November 1944, the 399th enters the front lines and begins its first combat activity: patrolling the flanks of the 3rd Infantry Division in a forest in the Vosges foothills.

"Nazi village" training pays off: One GI enters a house to begin a search for possible enemy soldiers while other GIs provide cover.

GIs of the 399th moving along a road through a rural French village in the Vosges.

Second Lieutenant Rudolph Steinman of the 399th receives a Distinguished Service Cross from General Wade Haislip for Tête des Reclos action—the Battlefield Commissions wore their bars in their pockets.

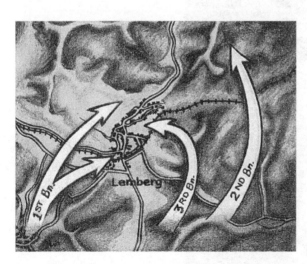

The 399th Infantry Regiment's pincers attack against Lemberg.

Major General Withers A. Burress, Commanding General, 100th Infantry Division (later Commanding General, 6th Corps, Seventh Army).

Brigadier General Andrew C. Tychsen, Commanding Officer, 399th Infantry Regiment (later Commanding General, 100th Infantry Division).

A 4F GOES TO WAR

American M4 Sherman medium tank on Shoenberg Ridge during the battle for Bitche.

A shell's eye view of Bitche. Americans coined a phrase.

Sons of Bitche: A jeep from H Company, 2nd Battalion, 399th Infantry Regiment, in Bitche.

GIs move cautiously through the destruction of Ludwigshafen.

Crossing the Neckar on rubber rafts, infantrymen enter Heilbronn. How the author arrived there, too.

Fox Company mops up along Adolf Hitler Strasse in Heilbronn.

The author receiving his Battlefield Commission from Maj. Gen. Withers A. Burress on 2 May 1945 at Bad Constadt, Germany.

The author in Paris, June 1945.

A 4F GOES TO WAR

The author after receiving the coveted National Order of Battlefield Commissions (NOBC) Commanders Trophy at San Antonio, Texas, September 1993.

The author and friend Bud Warnecke, a battalion commander with the 82nd Airborne Division on 6 June 1944, at NOBC Convention, September 1993.

A 4F Goes to War

Made in the USA
Monee, IL
30 March 2025

14872321R00069